GRIL COOKBOOK

THIS BOOK INCLUDES:

TREAGER GRILL BIBLE AND NINJA FOODI GRILL COOKBOOK

GRILL ACADEMY

© Copyright 2021 by GRILL ACADEMY All rights reserved.

The following Book is reproduced below with the goal of providing information that is as accurate and reliable as possible. Regardless, purchasing this Book can be seen as consent to the fact that both the publisher and the author of this book are in no way experts on the topics discussed within and that any recommendations or suggestions that are made herein are for entertainment purposes only. Professionals should be consulted as needed prior to undertaking any of the action endorsed herein.

This declaration is deemed fair and valid by both the American Bar Association and the Committee of Publishers Association and is legally binding throughout the United States.

Furthermore, the transmission, duplication, or reproduction of any of the following work including specific information will be considered an illegal act irrespective of if it is done electronically or in print. This extends to creating a secondary or tertiary copy of the work or a recorded copy and is only allowed with the express written consent from the Publisher. All additional right reserved.

The information in the following pages is broadly considered a truthful and accurate account of facts and as such, any inattention, use, or misuse of the information in question by the reader will render any resulting actions solely under their purview. There are no scenarios in which the publisher or the original author of this work can be in any fashion deemed liable for any hardship or damages that may befall them after undertaking information described herein.

Additionally, the information in the following pages is intended only for informational purposes and should thus be thought of as universal. As befitting its nature, it is presented without assurance regarding its prolonged validity or interim quality. Trademarks that are mentioned are done without written consent and can in no way be considered an endorsement from the trademark holder.

TRAEGER GRILL BIBLE

The guide to master your wood pellet grill with healthy and tasty recipes for beginners and advanced pitmasters

Grill Academy

© Copyright 2020 - All rights reserved.

The content contained within this book may not be reproduced, duplicated or transmitted without direct written permission from the author or the publisher. Under no circumstances will any blame or legal responsibility be held against the publisher, or author, for any damages, reparation, or monetary loss due to the information contained within this book. Either directly or indirectly.

Legal Notice:

This book is copyright protected. This book is only for personal use. You cannot amend, distribute, sell, use, quote or paraphrase any part, or the content within this book, without the consent of the author or publisher.

Disclaimer Notice:

Please note the information contained within this document is for educational and entertainment purposes only. All effort has been executed to present accurate, up to date, and reliable, complete information. No warranties of any kind are declared or implied. Readers acknowledge that the author is not engaging in the rendering of legal, financial, medical or professional advice. The content within this book has been derived from various sources. Please consult a licensed professional before attempting any techniques outlined in this book. By reading this document, the reader agrees that under no circumstances is the author responsible for any losses, direct or indirect, which are incurred as a result of the use of information contained within this document, including, but not limited to, errors, omissions, or inaccuracies.

TRAEGER GRILL BIBLE 4

INTRODUCTION 12
History of the Wood Pellet Smoker and Grill 12

WHAT IS THE TRAGER WOOD PELLET GRILL 14
What is a Traeger Grill? 14
Anatomy of a Pellet Grill 14
How Does It Work 16
What You Can Cook with Your Traeger 16
Why Choose Pellet Grill in Cooking? 17
The Advantages of Traeger Grill 18

TIPS AND TRICKS TO MAKE 20
Do Not Lose Patience 20
Placing the Meat 20
The Pre-Heat 20
Using the Right Tools 20
Marinating is the Key 21
Temperatures for Different Foods 21
Times and Doneness 22
Different Flavors for Pellet 23

HOW TO CLEAN THE TRAEGER GRILL AFTER USE 24

BEEF RECIPES 26

PORK RECIPES 47

SEAFOOD RECIPES 63

VEGETARIAN RECIPES 81

VEGAN RECIPES 99

POULTRY RECIPES 109

EXTRA RECIPES 131

CONCLUSION 151

NINJA FOODI GRILL 154

INTRODUCTION	158
THE GRILL GRATE	158
CRISPER BASKET	159
PROS OF USING NINJA FOODI GRILL	159
NINJA FOODI GRILL UNBOXING	160
CHAPTER 2 WHAT IS NINJA FOODI GRILL?	162
NINJA FOODI FUNCTIONALITIES	162
HOW TO USE THE NINJA FOODI GRILL	166
GRILLING	166
ROASTING	167
BAKING	167
AIR FRYING / AIR CRISPING	167
DEHYDRATING	167
COOKING FROZEN FOODS	167
CLEANING AND MAINTENANCE	168
TROUBLESHOOTING	168
CHAPTER 3 BREAKFAST	170
1. GRILLED FRENCH TOAST	170
2. SAUSAGE WITH EGGS	172
3. ESPRESSO GLAZED BAGELS	173
4. BRUSCHETTA PORTOBELLO MUSHROOMS	174
5. SAUSAGE MIXED GRILL	175
6. SAUSAGE AND EGG LOADED BREAKFAST POCKETS	176
7. GRILLED CINNAMON TOAST WITH BERRIES AND WHIPPED CREAM	178
8. AVOCADO EGGS	180
9. COCONUT FRENCH TOAST	181
10. BACON-HERB GRIT	182
CHAPTER 4 SNACKS	184
1. CRISPY BRUSSELS LEAVES	184
2. CAJUNED EGGPLANT APPETIZER	186
3. GRILLED HONEY CARROTS	187
4. MOLTEN LAVA CAKES	188
5. FRIED OREOS	189

- 6. CHOCOLATE CHIP COOKIE 190
- 7. BLUEBERRY HAND PIES 191
- 8. CHERRY JAM TARTS 192
- 9. BROWNIE BARS 194

CHAPTER 5   BEEF AND PORK 197

- 1. BOURBON PORK CHOPS 197
- 2. KOREAN CHILI PORK 198
- 3. LETTUCE CHEESE STEAK 199
- 4. GRILLED BEEF BURGERS 200
- 5. ESPRESSO MARINATED CHILI STEAK 202
- 6. KOREAN CHILI PORK 203
- 7. MUSTARD DREDGED PORK 204
- 8. JAMAICAN PORK DISH 205
- 9. TANTALIZING BEEF JERKY 206
- 10. SPICY ADOBO STEAK 207
- 11. BEEF STEW 208
- 12. LAMB ROAST 209
- 13. MUSTARD PORK 210

CHAPTER 6   FISH AND SEAFOOD 211

- 1. SUBTLY ROASTED BBQ SHRIMP 211
- 2. CAPER SAUCE DREDGED SWORD FISH 213
- 3. COOL AND SPICY SHRIMP 214
- 4. TERIYAKI SALMON AND VEGETABLES 215
- 5. SHRIMP AND VEGETABLE EGG ROLLS 216
- 6. CLAM CHOWDER WITH PARMESAN CRACKERS 218
- 7. CRAB AND ROASTED ASPARAGUS RISOTTO 220
- 8. THAI FISH CURRY 222
- 9. BLACKENED SALMON WITH CREAMY GRITS 224
- 10. SALMON CAKES 226

CHAPTER 7   POULTRY 230

- 1. HEARTY CHICKEN ZUCCHINI KABOBS 230
- 2. SWEET AND SOUR CHICKEN BBQ 232
- 3. DELICIOUS MAPLE GLAZED CHICKEN 233
- 4. HOT AND SASSY BBQ CHICKEN 234

5. MOROCCAN ROAST CHICKEN 235
6. CLASSIC HONEY SOY CHICKEN 236
7. NINJA FOODI BBQ GRILLED CHICKEN 237
8. NINJA FOODI CRACK BBQ CHICKEN 238
9. NINJA FOODI STICKY GRILLED CHICKEN 239
10. NINJA FOODI GRILLED CHICKEN BREAST 240
11. NINJA FOODI GRILLED PINEAPPLE CHICKEN 241
12. NINJA FOODI GRILLED CHICKEN WINGS 242

CHAPTER 8 VEGETARIAN 243

1. VEGETABLE PASTA DELIGHT 243
2. CREAMY CORN POTATOES 246
3. SPINACH CHICKPEA STEW 248
4. CHEESE STUFFED ZUCCHINI 250
5. BROCCOLI CRISP 251
6. MASHED ASPARAGUS 252
7. APPLE GREEN SALAD 253
8. SPINACH OLIVE MEAL 254

CHAPTER 9 DESSERTS 255

1. CREAMY MANGO CAKE 255
2. EASY PINEAPPLE CAKE 256
3. CHOCOLATE PUDDING 258
4. CHOCOLATE PEANUT BUTTER AND JELLY PUFFS 259
5. RED VELVET CHEESECAKE 261
6. BLACK BEANS BROWNIES 261
7. COCOA AND ORANGE PUDDING 263
8. APPLE PIE 264
9. APPLE JAM 265
10. PINEAPPLE AND YOGURT CAKE 266

CHAPTER 10 EXTRA RECIPES 267

1. TOMATO SALSA 267
2. POTATO CORN CHOWDER 268
3. MUSHROOM TOMATO ROAST 269
4. CHEDDAR CAULIFLOWER MEAL 270
5. BUTTERY SPINACH MEAL 271

6. Turkey Dip 272
7. Sweet Potato Dip 273
8. Apple Dip 274
9. Orange Cranberry Dip 275
10. Chili Basil Dip 276

CONCLUSION 277

Introduction

With so many grills available in the market, the Traeger Grill is considered one of the top-of-the-line grills that you can ever invest in for your outdoor kitchen. This innovative grill allows you to cook authentic grilled foods. However, you do not deviate from the tradition of cooking using wood pellets so you do not get that distasteful aftertaste you get from cooking in a gas grill.

Made by an Oregon-based company, the Traeger Grill has been around for many decades. This type of smoker grill is known to cook food using all-nature wood pellets so that foods smell and taste great and healthy. However, unlike traditional smokers, the Traeger Grill has been innovated to provide convenience even to grill and barbecue neophytes. It comes with a motor that turns the drill and thus consistently feeding the burn pot so you can achieve even cooking.

History of the Wood Pellet Smoker and Grill

The very first Wood Pellet Smoker-Grill was introduced in 1985. Joe Traeger was the man behind the concept and the construction of the Wood Pellet Smoker-Grill. After spending a year creating his smoker-grill, he obtained a patent and started production at a commercial level. The smoker-grill looked similar to traditional smokers in terms of its exterior design. There was a drum barrel and a chimney. But the internal components were the true magic. Traeger divided the internal design into three parts. These three parts were the sections where wood pellets had to go in order to get burned.

The storage hopper was the first part, which worked as storage for the wood pellets in the smoker-grill. Then, the next stop for the pellets was the auger, which was a rotating section. This rotation allowed wood pellets to reach the third and final section. This final section was called a firebox or burning box. In this area, a fan allowed the proper distribution of the cultivated heat.

In the early designs, the user had to light the smoker-grill manually. However, the design got updated with time, and now, there are completely automatic Wood Pellet Smoker-Grills available.

The reduction in wood pellet size revolutionized the whole smoking and grilling process. The machine obtained the ability to balance the temperatures on its own for as long as required. This convenience wasn't available with charcoal burning smokers. At the same time, wood pellets also provided more variety based on the flavorful hardwood choices available.

That would not be wrong to say that the BBQ world experienced a revolution with the introduction of the Wood Pellet Smoker-Grill. Cooking got simpler and more comfortable, which gave even newbies a chance to smoke, grill, bake, and roast. The machine was capable of handling the temperature on its own, so the users could be stress-free and safe when cooking. In 2007, after the expiration of Traeger's patent, the Wood Pellet Smoker-Grill market opened for more advanced options. This led to more advancements and automation in the equipment.

CHAPTER 1:

What Is the Trager Wood Pellet Grill

What is a Traeger Grill?

Traeger Wood Pellet Grills are electric grills that use wood pellets as their fuel source. The specially designed wood pellets can also be used as flavor enhancers to give food an excellent smoky taste. With his grill, Joe Traeger revolutionized barbecuing and made it convenient and straightforward. Traeger Wood Pellet Grill and Smoker does not require constant monitoring and can leave to regulate itself while cooking.

There are five methods of cooking with the grill; they include:

- Indirect grilling
- Direct grilling
- Smoking
- Roasting
- Baking

Despite fierce competition, Traeger grills continue to be the world's No 1 best-selling wood pellet grill because of its mastery of the wood-fired cooking craft. The grill is capable of transforming a simple fare into an extraordinary dish with its wood-fired flavoring. The grill temperatures can range from 150°F to well over 375°F to enable it to grill, sear, roast, smoke, and bake. It produces consistent results.

Anatomy of a Pellet Grill

The Hopper

On the side of the pellet grill you'll find a hopper, which houses your supply of wood pellets. Hopper size varies based on which model of pellet grill you own, but most hold between 10 and 20 pounds of wood pellets at a time.

The hopper has its own lid and can be accessed mid cook without opening the lid of your cooking chamber. This way, you can maintain the ambient temperature of your grill even if you need to refill wood pellets in the middle of your cook.

The Digital Controller

The digital controller is what gives pellet grills their ease of use and precision. With the turn of a dial or the press of a button, you can set your temperature just like you would on a traditional oven. An LED display will show your grill's actual temperature so you can know exactly how your food is being cooked.

A sensor probe inside your grill monitors the cooker's ambient temperature. If the temperature falls too low, the controller will distribute more wood pellets down to the fire pot to ignite. This is part of what makes pellet grills so easy to use - they automate temperature management.

Many newer pellet grill models also have built-in probe thermometers, which are one of the most important tools for any grill master. Built-in thermometers will display your food's internal temperature on the LED display alongside your grill's ambient temperature.

The Auger

Pellets that are dispensed by the digital controller fall down into an auger, which is a screw-shaped design feature. The auger rotates in place and pushes pellets forward to be fed into the firepot.

The Firepot

After the wood pellets journey through the auger, they are dumped into a firepot. In the firepot, an electric igniter rod heats pellets until they begin to smolder, smoke, and ignite.

Just above the firepot is a deflector plate that distributes heat around the grill. The deflector plate eliminates hot spots and also acts as a shield for the firepot. No drippings, fats, grease, or oils can make their way to the firepot – completely eliminating the possibility of flare-ups.

The Fan

Pellet grills also come with a built-in fan system to feed oxygen to the firepot. After all, there's no fire without oxygen.

When more heat is required, the digital controller will turn the fan cadence up to increase oxygen flow. This principle is pretty similar in nature to how air dampers and vents work in charcoal grills and smokers.

The Chimney

Typically, on the opposite end from the hopper there's a chimney that allows smoke to exit the cooking chamber. This creates a draw of airflow to keep heat and smoke flowing properly inside of the cooking chamber. It's also an escape for smoke so that you don't over-smoke your food.

How Does It Work

Wood pellet smokers and grills are basically outdoor cookers that run on electricity. Once the digital controller is turned on, a rotator auger delivers wood pellets to the fire pot that features an igniter rod. The igniter rod then heats the pellets for some time. This causes the pellets to combust, produce smoke and heat that are then diffused with the help of a fan.

What You Can Cook with Your Traeger

There is no actual limit to the recipes you can cook like chicken, hot dogs, vegetables, seafood, chicken, brisket, rabbit, turkey, and even more. The cooking process is very easy; all you have to do is to pack your favorite wood pellets into the hopper, then program the temperature you desire on the controller, then place the food on the pellet Smoker and Grill. That is, it and the pellet will be able to maintain the temperature and keep the pellets burning.

Pellet Smoker and Grills are characterized by being electric, and it requires a usual standard outlet of about 110v so that you can power the digital board, fan, and auger.

There is a wide variety of types of pellet smokers and grills, like electric pellet smokers, wood fired grills, wood pellet grills, and wood pellet smokers, to name a few pellet Smoker and Grill names. But all these names refer to the same outdoor cooker appliance that is only fueled by hardwood pellets. And there are many brands of Wood Pellet Smoker and Grills, like Traeger.

Why Choose Pellet Grill in Cooking?

Cooking on a pellet grill is a new and unique experience. By utilizing hardwood pellets, the meat product is infused with a very woodsy, smoky flavor. The new Pellet Smoker Grills can be relied on to do the work on their own, as they are set up to be automatic by the user.

The main and most obvious difference is that they provide the user with an automated air and fuel delivery system, making a pellet grill much more comfortable to control temperatures and relax while doing it.

So, if you thought that smokers are just too challenging to control cooking temperatures, well, think again. Pellet grills simply remove the fuss and worry that traditional smokers require, making them virtually a "set it and forget it" way to grill.

Pellet grills give you even more, as if that were not enough. With your new pellet grill, you have the absolute convenience of combining several varied cooking options. Old-time smokers only smoke their food, so if you want to grill, bake, and roast your food, you would need to purchase separate units for each process.

Pellet Grills are different from propane or gas grills in that they offer more control. Pellet grills and gas grills both offer their own set of convenient features to the outdoor chef but look more closely, and you will see some major differences. Gas grills are very good when cooking chores, but due to poor insulation, they do not typically perform very well at all at low cooking temperatures. In addition, the older style of propane grills needs to be set up so that they receive the proper degree of ventilation. This, alone, makes them a poor choice for smokers. The Pellet Grill is a no-brainer in today's world!

Pellet grills provide the chef with more flavor options. With pellet grills, the wood pellets are available in many different flavors. This provides you with the ability to cook all the foods on your Pellet Smoker Grill. In the end, sure, they both cook your food, but the pellet grill is exponentially better on so many levels. For me, there is no choice but to the Pellet Smoker Grill!

Then there is the question of using a Pellet Grill or staying with the highly coveted charcoal method of barbecuing your fine foods.

Charcoal grills have long been considering the king of the backyard barbecue area. There are several choices of configurations for charcoal grills but with two choices for fuel: lump charcoal or charcoal briquettes. Grilling using a charcoal grill is definitely a labor of love. I know several people who defend them to the ends of the earth, and that is fine. We are different, and thank goodness for that, too. However, cooking on a charcoal grill is not so easy. It takes quite a lot of practice to get all the elements just right, and it is difficult to control temperatures.

The way pellet grills are used when grilling and smoking are infinitely simpler. This is exactly why they have become the nation's number one seller. As for the cleanup, have you ever seen a charcoal grill the next morning? You may need to carry them out to the trash or recycling. It is not the same with your pellet grill, though.

The Advantages of Traeger Grill

The Traeger Grill is not only limited to, well, grilling. It is an essential outdoor kitchen appliance as it allows you to also bake, roast, and smoke, braise, and barbecue. Nevertheless, more than being a useful kitchen appliance, below are the advantages of getting your very own Traeger Grill:

- **Better flavor:** The Traeger Grill uses all-natural wood, so food comes out better tasting than when you cook them in a gas or charcoal grill. You can impart 14 different flavors to your food. This book will have its chapter dedicated to those 14 flavors of pellets.

- **No flare-ups:** No flare-ups mean that food is cooked evenly on all sides. This is possible by using indirect heat. Because there are no flare-ups, you can smoke, bake, and rose without some areas or sides of your food burning.

- **Mechanical parts are well designed and protected:** The mechanical parts of the Traeger Grill protected particularly from fats and drippings, so it is not stuck over time.

- **Exceptional temperature control:** The Traeger Grill has exceptional temperature control. The thing is that all you need is to set up the heat, and the grill will maintain a consistent temperature even if the weather goes bad. Moreover, having a stable temperature control allows you to cook food better and tastier minus the burnt taste.

- **Built-in Wi-Fi:** All Traeger Grills have built-in Wi-Fi to set them up, even if you are not physically present in front of your grill. Moreover, the grill also alerts you once your food is ready. With this setting, you will be able to do other important things instead of slaving in front of your grill. Lastly, it also comes with an app that allows you to check many recipes from their website.

- **Environmentally friendly:** Perhaps the main selling point of the Traeger Grill is that it is environmentally friendly. Traeger Grill uses all-natural wood pellets, so your grill does not produce harmful chemicals when you are using it… only smoky goodness.

The thing is that the Traeger Grill is more than just your average grill. It is one of the best, and you will get your money's worth with this grill.

CHAPTER 2:

Tips and Tricks to Make the Best Use of the Traeger Grill

Even if you are a novice who lacks enough experience when it comes to BBQ, I am here to share some of the best tips and tricks with you. After you have gone through this chapter, you will be in a better place to make much better meals and become a pro at using BBQ.

Do Not Lose Patience

It is very important to be patient when you are cooking. Do not be in a rush when you are barbecuing, as the authentic taste only comes when you allow the meat to be cook slowly and thoroughly.

Placing the Meat

When you are looking for a barbecue, it is very important to learn the right placement of meat. If you put the meat on the grill immediately on heating the flame, it is likely to be scorch on the outside, and the sides will not cook well. You can do this for steaks but anything else; put them on the grill after the flames have died down. The will produce even cooking results.

The Pre-Heat

Do not take pre-heat lightly. Based on the chosen recipe, some of the sausages and other meat products may need to cook a little before transferring them to the grill. Alternately, after barbecuing them, they have to be placed on the baking tray as well. So, pay heed to these little factors thoroughly and meticulously.

Using the Right Tools

When you are looking to have a barbecue feast, there is absolutely no way you can be reckless with your choices. This is why regardless of the kind of expense it may entail; we want you to use the easy blend of tools when cooking. The kind of tongs you are using for flipping over the meat or any other product and anything else should be top-notch. Do not compromise with the tools and equipment as it all plays a role when it comes to the true taste of barbecue.

Marinating is the Key

As we have told, when it comes to barbecue, 'Authentic' is the watchword here. So, if a recipe says to add marinade, make sure you do that. Brushing the meat or even the fish with marinade every 10 to 15 minutes while it is cooking might be a great way to get the best result. Doing this adds moisture and traps the flavor of the smoke. This enhances the flavor a great deal. We are sure that you will love to barbecue owing to the kind of fun it is. Like we have mentioned before, choosing the right grill is crucial and always measures the amount of food you will have to make. The right calculations ensure that you will not have to repeat the effort multiple times. So, are you all set now to discover some of the finest recipes and the most lip-smacking dishes of all time? Don your chef's hat right away, as we dive deep into the world of the best of BBQ recipes that are bound to make you a connoisseur of food!

Temperatures for Different Foods

Raw: Some people do eat steak raw. You may hear this term used when referring to steak tartare, tiger meat

Rare: If you order your steaks rare, that means that you like the center to reach a warm to cool temperature. The texture on the inside will be soft and spongy. The internal temperature will reach 120 degrees.

Medium rare: A steak cooked to medium rare has an internal temperature of 126 degrees, so it is only slightly warmer than a steak cooked to rare. This steak will have a hot outside and a warm red center.

Well done: If you are the type of person that does not like any pink on the inside of your meat, then you probably want your steak cooked well done. A well-done steak has an internal temperature of 160 degrees and is completely cooked on the inside.

Times and Doneness

Type of Meat	USDA Recommended Temperature	Doneness Preference
Whole Beef Steak, Prime Rib, etc.	**145°F** + 3 Minute Rest	Rare - 125°F Medium Rare - 130°F Medium - 140°F Medium Well - 150°F Well Done - 160°F
Ground Beef Hamburger, Meatloaf, etc.	**160°F**	Medium Rare - 130°F Medium - 140°F Medium Well - 150°F Well Done - 160°F
Pork Ham, Chops, Roast, ect.	**145°F** + 3 Minute Rest	Medium - 145°F Medium Well - 155°F Well Done - 160°F
Poultry Chicken, Turkey, Duck, etc.	**165°F**	
Lamb Roast, Chops, etc.	**145°F** + 3 Minute Rest	Rare - 125°F Medium Rare - 130°F Medium - 140°F Medium Well - 150°F Well Done - 160°F
Veal Chops, etc.	**145°F** + 3 Minute Rest	Rare - 125°F Medium Rare - 130°F Medium - 140°F Medium Well - 150°F Well Done - 160°F
Fish & Shellfish Cod, Salmon, Tilapia, Lobster, Shrimp, ect.	**145°F**	

Different Flavors for Pellet

1. Wood	2. Flavor Profile	3. Use With
4. Alder	5. Delicate and earthy, with a hint of sweetness	6. Fish, Shellfish, Beef, Pork, Lamb, Poultry, Veggies
7. Apple	8. Mild, subtle sweet and fruity flavor	9. Pork, Poultry, Lamb, Wild Game, Beef, Some Seafood
10. Cherry	11. Light and sweet. Delicate, not overpowering	12. Beef, Pork, Poultry, Wild Game, Some Seafood
13. Hickory	14. Sweet, yet strong flavor. Not overpowering. Versatile	15. Beef, Pork, Poultry, Fish, Wild Game
16. Maple	17. Mild and slightly sweet flavor	18. Beef, Pork, Poultry, Small Game Birds, Cheese, Veggies
19. Mesquite	20. Strong and earthy flavor. One of the hottest burning woods	21. Red meats, Dark Meats, Wild Game
22. Oak	23. Medium smoky flavor. Versatile. Milder than Hickory, stronger than Cherry	24. Beef, Pork, Poultry, Fish, Some Wild Game
25. Pecan	26. Stronger than most fruitwoods, but milder than Hickory and Mesquite	27. Beef, Pork, Poultry
28. Peach	29. Sweet, fruity flavor	30. Pork, Poultry, Small Game Birds

CHAPTER 3:

How to Clean the Traeger Grill After Use

Traeger grills are easy to clean compare to similar grills. You would need to clean it every five uses, which is wonderful. Traditional grills can be a chore to clean and can get pretty grimy quickly. Luckily, the Traeger's design allows you to get your grill ready for the next cook-out in a few simple steps.

1. Open the grill lid and wipe the grates with a paper towel or damp cloth. If your grates have more residue, you can use a grill mark brush instead. Use a scraper to remove debris at the back wall of the grill, then let all the dirt fall on the bottom of the drip tray.

2. Brush or wipe the inside of the smoke exhaust and empty the grease bucket.

3. Take out the drip pan and replace it with a fresh aluminum foil.

4. Siphon the ash beneath the heat deflector and on the inside of the fire pot using a vacuum.

5. Use a grease cleaner or soapy water on a spray bottle for cleaning the exterior of the grill. Spray it while carefully avoiding the electronic controls. Leave it on for 1 minute, then wipe it down with a clean cloth.

More Tips:

- Make sure that the grill has completely cooled down before cleaning.
- Take the opportunity to visually inspect the parts when cleaning to have it in excellent working order.
- Follow the top to bottom cleaning method.

- Empty the pellet hopper and vacuum the insides to get any ash or dust.
- You may need to clean the temperature probes when they get grubby. Do these gently by using a clean, damp cloth.
- Be careful when drawing out the grate since you may damage or scrape the temperature probe.
- Always replace the foil every cook cycle to keep the smoke flavors pristine and avoid getting any particulates from previous cooks sticking to what you are currently grilling.
- Use grease liners or aluminum foil for the grease bucket for easy cleanup. Never pour the grease down the drain since this will clog your pipes.

CHAPTER 4:

Beef Recipes

Smoked Midnight Brisket

Preparation Time: 15 minutes

Cooking Time: 12 hours

Servings: 6

Ingredients:

- 1 Tablespoon Worcestershire sauce
- 1 Tablespoon Traeger beef Rub
- 1 Tablespoon Traeger Chicken rub
- 1 Tablespoon Traeger Blackened Saskatchewan rub
- 5 lb flat cut brisket

- 1 cup beef broth

Directions:
1. Rub the sauce and rubs in a mixing bowl, then rub the mixture on the meat.
2. Preheat your grill to 180°F with the lid closed for 15 minutes. You can use super smoke if you desire.
3. Place the meat on the grill and grill for 6 hours or until the internal temperature reaches 160°F.
4. Remove the meat from the grill and double wrap it with foil.

5. Add beef broth and return to grill with the temperature increased to 225°F. Cook for 4 hours or until the internal temperature reaches 204°F.
6. Remove from grill and let rest for 30 minutes. Serve and enjoy with your favorite BARBECUE sauce.

Nutrition:

- Calories 200,
- Total fat 14g,
- Protein 14g,
- Sugar 0g,
- Fiber 0g,
- Sodium: 680mg

Smoked Beef Ribs

Preparation Time: 25 minutes

Cooking Time: 4 to 6 hours

Servings: 4 to 8

Ingredients:

- 2 (2- or 3-pound) racks beef ribs
- 2 tablespoons yellow mustard
- 1 batch Sweet and Spicy Cinnamon Rub

Directions:

1. Supply your smoker with wood pellets and follow the manufacturer's specific start-up procedure. Allow your griller to preheat with the lid closed to 225°F.
2. Take off the membrane from the backside of the ribs. This can be done by cutting just through the membrane in an X pattern and working a paper towel between the membrane and the ribs to pull it off.
3. Coat the ribs all over with mustard and season them with the rub. Using your two hands, work with the rub into the meat.
4. Put your ribs directly on the grill grate and smoke until their internal temperature reaches between 190°F and 200°F.
5. Remove the racks from the grill and cut them into individual ribs. Serve immediately.

Nutrition:

- Calories: 230
- Carbs: 0g
- Fat: 17g
- Protein: 20g

Traeger Beef Jerky

Preparation Time: 15 minutes

Cooking Time: 5 hours

Servings: 10

Ingredients:

- 3 pounds sirloin steaks
- 2 cups soy sauce
- 1 cup pineapple juice
- 1/2 cup brown sugar
- 2 tbsp sriracha
- 2 tbsp hoisin
- 2 tbsp red pepper flake
- 2 tbsp rice wine vinegar
- 2 tbsp onion powder

Directions:

1. Mix the marinade in a zip lock bag and add the beef. Mix until well coated and remove as much air as possible.
2. Place the bag in a fridge and let marinate overnight or for 6 hours. Remove the bag from the fridge an hour prior to cooking
3. Startup the Traeger and set it on the smoking settings or at 190F.
4. Lay the meat on the grill, leaving a half-inch space between the pieces. Let cool for 5 hours and turn after 2 hours.
5. Remove from the grill and let cool. Serve or refrigerate

Nutrition:

- Calories: 309 Cal Fat: 7 g Carbohydrates: 20 g
- Protein: 34 g Fiber: 1 g

Traeger Smoked Beef Roast

Preparation Time: 10 minutes

Cooking Time: 6 hours

Servings: 6

Ingredients:

- 1-3/4 pounds beef sirloin tip roast
- 1/2 cup barbeque rub
- 2 bottles amber beer
- 1 bottle BBQ sauce

Directions:

1. Turn the Traeger onto the smoke setting.
2. Rub the beef with barbeque rub until well coated, then place on the grill. Let smoke for 4 hours while flipping every 1 hour.
3. Transfer the beef to a pan and add the beer. The beef should be 1/2 way covered.
4. Braise the beef until fork tender. It will take 3 hours on the stovetop and 60 minutes on the instant pot.
5. Remove the beef from the ban and reserve 1 cup of the cooking liquid.
6. Use 2 forks to shred the beef into small pieces, then return to the pan with the reserved braising liquid. Add BBQ sauce and stir well, then keep warm until serving. You can also reheat if it gets cold.

Nutrition:

- Calories: 829 Cal Fat: 18 g
- Carbohydrates: 4 g Protein: 86 g Fiber: 0 g

Reverse Seared Flank Steak

Preparation Time: 10 minutes

Cooking Time: 20 minutes

Servings: 2

Ingredients:

- 3 pound flank steaks
- 1 tbsp salt
- 1/2 tbsp onion powder
- 1/4 tbsp garlic powder
- 1/2 black pepper, coarsely ground

Directions:

1. Preheat the Traeger to 225F.
2. Add the steaks and rub them generously with the rub mixture.
3. Place the steak
4. Let cook until its internal temperature is 100F under your desired temperature. 115F for rare, 125F for the medium rear, and 135F for medium.
5. Wrap the steak with foil and raise the grill temperature to high. Place back the steak and grill for 3 minutes on each side.
6. Pat with butter and serve when hot.

Nutrition:

- Calories: 112 Cal
- Fat: 5 g
- Carbohydrates: 1 g
- Protein: 16 g
- Fiber: 0 g

Traeger New York Strip

Preparation Time: 5 minutes

Cooking Time: 15 minutes

Servings: 6

Ingredients:

- 3 New York strips
- Salt and pepper

Directions:

1. If the steak is in the fridge, remove it 30 minutes prior to cooking.
2. Preheat the Traeger to 450F.
3. Meanwhile, season the steak generously with salt and pepper. Place it on the grill and let it cook for 5 minutes per side or until the internal temperature reaches 128F.
4. Rest for 10 minutes.

Nutrition:

- Calories: 198 Cal
- Fat: 14 g
- Carbohydrates: 0 g
- Protein: 17 g
- Fiber: 0 g

Traeger Stuffed Peppers

Preparation Time: 20 minutes

Cooking Time: 5 minutes

Servings: 6

Ingredients:

- 3 bell peppers, sliced in halves
- 1 pound ground beef, lean
- 1 onion, chopped
- 1/2 tbsp red pepper flakes
- 1/2 tbsp salt
- 1/4 tbsp pepper
- 1/2 tbsp garlic powder
- 1/2 tbsp onion powder
- 1/2 cup white rice
- 15 oz stewed tomatoes
- 8 oz tomato sauce
- 6 cups cabbage, shredded
- 1-1/2 cup water
- 2 cups cheddar cheese

Directions:

1. Arrange the pepper halves on a baking tray and set aside.
2. Preheat your grill to 325F.
3. Brown the meat in a large skillet. Add onions, pepper flakes, salt, pepper, garlic, and onion, and cook until the meat is well cooked.

4. Add rice, stewed tomatoes, tomato sauce, cabbage, and water. Cover and simmer until the rice is well cooked, the cabbage is tender, and there is no water in the rice.
5. Place the cooked beef mixture in the pepper halves and top with cheese.
6. Place in the grill and cook for 30 minutes.
7. Serve immediately and enjoy it.

Nutrition:

- Calories: 422 Cal
- Fat: 22 g
- Carbohydrates: 24 g
- Protein: 34 g
- Fiber: 5 g

Beef Tenderloin

Preparation Time: 10 minutes

Cooking Time: 30 minutes

Servings: 8

Ingredients:

- 4 pounds beef tenderloin
- 1 tablespoon olive oil
- ½ teaspoon paprika
- 2 teaspoon Jacobsen salt
- ½ teaspoon ground cumin
- 1 teaspoon red pepper flakes
- 1 teaspoon ground black pepper
- 1 teaspoon fresh thyme
- ½ teaspoon oregano

Mustard Cream Sauce:

- 1 teaspoon freshly ground black pepper
- 1 teaspoon oil
- 1 cup heavy cream
- ¼ cup shallot (chopped)
- 2 teaspoon chopped fresh basil
- 2 teaspoon chopped fresh dill
- 1 garlic clove (minced)
- 1 cup dry white wine
- 4 tablespoon mustard
- 1 teaspoon Jacobsen salt

Directions:

1. In a small mixing bowl, combine the thyme, oregano, pepper flakes, black pepper, cumin, salt, paprika, and oregano.
2. Rub all sides of the tenderloin with olive oil.
3. Sprinkle rub mixture over the tenderloin as needed. Make sure the tenderloin is coated in seasonings.
4. Preheat your pellet smoker grill on HIGH with the lid closed. Use apple or maple wood pellet.
5. Place tenderloin on the grill grate and cook for about 15 minutes.
6. Reduce the grill temperature to 375°F and cook for an additional 30 minutes or until the tenderloin's temperature reaches 130°F.
7. Remove the tenderloin from heat and let it rest for a few minutes to cool.
8. For the mustard sauce, heat up the olive oil in a saucepan over medium to high heat.
9. Add the shallot and garlic. Saute until the veggies are tender.
10. Stir in the mustard, black pepper, and wine.
11. Bring to a boil, reduce the heat and simmer until the sauce thickens, stirring often.
12. Remove the saucepan from heat and stir in the heavy cream, basil, dill, salt, and pepper.
13. Cut the tenderloin into sizes and serve with mustard sauce.

Nutrition:

- Carbohydrates: 12 g
- Protein: 28 g
- Fat: 16 g
- Sodium: 23 mg
- Cholesterol: 21 mg

Beef Stuffed Bell Pepper

Preparation Time: 10 minutes

Cooking Time: 30 minutes

Servings: 8

Ingredients:

- 4 large red bell pepper
- ½ cups cooked rice
- 1 small onion (diced)
- 1 teaspoon chili powder
- 1 tomato (finely chopped)
- 1 teaspoon olive oil
- ¼ teaspoon ground black pepper or to taste
- ¼ teaspoon red pepper flakes
- ½ teaspoon salt
- ¼ teaspoon garlic
- 1-pound ground beef
- 1 cup shredded parmesan cheese
- 4 tablespoon ketchup
- ½ cup dry quick oats

Directions:

1. Cut off the top of the pepper and scoop out the pepper membrane and seeds.
2. Heat up the olive oil in a large skillet over medium to high heat. Add the onion and sliced tomatoes. Saute until the onion is tender.
3. Add the ground beef and cook until the ground beef is pink, breaking the beef apart while cooking.

4. Remove the skillet from heat and stir in the salt, garlic, ketchup, pepper, rice, oat, pepper flakes, and chili powder.
5. Start the grill on a smoker mode and leave open for 5 minutes or until the fire has started.
6. Close the lid and preheat it to 350°F, using mesquite wood pellet.
7. Arrange the stuffed pepper on the grill grate, stuffed side up. Cook stuffed peppers for about 40 minutes.
8. Top each stuffed pepper with parmesan cheese and cook for an additional 5 minutes or until the cheese is melted.

Nutrition:
- Carbohydrates: 32 g
- Protein: 18 g
- Fat: 6 g
- Sodium: 12 mg
- Cholesterol: 151 mg

Braised Beef Short Ribs

Preparation Time: 10 minutes

Cooking Time: 50 minutes

Servings: 8

Ingredients:

- 2 tablespoon olive oil
- 1 carrot (chopped)
- 2 red bell pepper (sliced)
- 1 onion (chopped)
- 2 tablespoon balsamic vinegar
- 4 pounds beef short ribs
- ½ teaspoon pepper
- 2 cups red wine
- 3 cups beef broth
- 1 teaspoon thyme
- ½ teaspoon paprika
- ½ teaspoon garlic powder
- 1 teaspoon salt or to taste
- ½ teaspoon onion powder
- 2 teaspoon dried peppermint

Directions:

1. Configure your wood pellet grill to smoke mode and leave the grill lid opened until the fire starts.
2. Close the lid and preheat grill to HIGH with the lid closed for 15 minutes, use apple or maple wood pellet.
3. Season all sides of the short rib generously with salt, onion powder, garlic powder, and pepper. Place the rib on the grill

grate and smoke for 10 minutes or until the rib is browned. Turn ribs after the first 5 minutes.

4. Remove the ribs from the grill and reduce the heat to 350°F.
5. Heat up the olive oil in a large Dutch grill over medium to high heat.
6. Add the onion, celery, and garlic. Saute for about 4 minutes or until the veggies are tender and fragrant. Stir constantly.
7. Add the tomato, carrot, bay leaves, and red bell pepper. Cook for 6 minutes, stirring often.
8. Pour in the red wine and balsamic vinegar. Stir to combine. Cook until the sauce thickens.
9. Pour in the beef broth and stir in the paprika, peppermint, and thyme.
10. Cover the Dutch grill tightly with aluminum foil and place it on the grill.
11. Braise at 350°F for 3 hours or until the meat is fork tender.
12. Remove the Dutch grill from heat and let the ribs sit for a few minutes to cool.
13. Use a slotted spoon to transfer the beef to a bowl. Close the bowl and set aside.
14. Stain the broth through a fine-mesh strainer. Press the vegetables to the mesh with a flat spoon to extract all juice.
15. Transfer the juice to a Dutch grill. Bring to a boil over medium to high heat. Reduce heat and simmer until the sauce thickens and has reduced by half.
16. Add the short ribs to the sauce and cook for 1 minute.
17. Remove the Dutch grill from heat.
18. Serve and enjoy.

Nutrition:

- Carbohydrates: 32 g Protein: 18 g Fat: 6 g
- Sodium: 12 mg Cholesterol: 151 mg

Almond Crusted Beef Fillet

Preparation Time: 15 minutes

Cooking Time: 55 minutes

Servings: 4

Ingredients:

- ¼ cup chopped almonds
- 1 tablespoon Dijon mustard
- 1 Cup chicken broth
- Salt
- 1/3 cup chopped onion
- ¼ cup olive oil
- Pepper
- 2 tablespoons curry powder
- 3 pounds beef fillet tenderloin

Directions:

1. Rub the pepper and salt into the tenderloin.
2. Place the almonds, mustard, chicken broth, curry, onion, and olive oil into a bowl. Stir well to combine.
3. Take this mixture and rub the tenderloin generously with it.
4. Add wood pellets to your smoker and follow your cooker's startup procedure. Preheat your smoker, with your lid closed, until it reaches 450.
5. Lay on the grill, cover, and smoke for ten minutes on both sides. Continue to cook until it reaches your desired doneness.
6. Take it all off the grill and let it rest for at least ten minutes.

Nutrition:

- Calories: 118 Carbs: 3g Fat: 3g Protein: 20g

Grilled Butter Basted Porterhouse Steak

Preparation Time: 15 minutes

Cooking Time: 40 minutes

Servings: 4

Ingredients:

- 4 Tablespoon butter, melted
- 2 Tablespoon Worcestershire sauce
- 2 Tablespoon Dijon mustard
- Traeger Prime rib rub

Directions:

1. Set your wood pellet grill to 225°F with the lid closed for 15 minutes.
2. In a mixing bowl, mix butter, sauce, dijon mustard until smooth. Brush the mixture on the meat, then season with the rub.
3. Arrange the meat on the grill grate and cook for 30 minutes.
4. Use tongs to transfer the meat to a patter, then increase the heat to high.
5. Return the meat to the grill grate to grill until your desired doneness is achieved.
6. Baste with the butter mixture again if you desire and let rest for 3 minutes before serving. Enjoy.

Nutrition:

- Calories 726, Total fat 62g,
- Protein 36g, Sugar 1g,
- Fiber 1g, Sodium: 97mg,

Wood Pellet Grill Prime Rib Roast

Preparation Time: 5 minutes

Cooking Time: 4 hours

Servings: 10

Ingredients:

- 7 lb bone prime rib roast
- Traeger prime rib rub

Directions:

1. Coat the roast generously with the rub, then wrap it in a plastic wrap. Let sit in the fridge for 24 hours to marinate.
2. Set the temperatures to 500°F.to to preheat with the lid closed for 15 minutes.
3. Place the rib directly on the grill fat side up and cook for 30 minutes.
4. Reduce the temperature to 300°F and cook for 4 hours or until the internal temperature is 120°F- rare, 130°F-medium rare, 140°F-medium and 150°F-well done.
5. Remove from the grill and let rest for 30 minutes, then serve and enjoy.

Nutrition:

- Calories 290,
- Total fat 23g,
- Protein 19g,
- Sugar 0g,
- Fiber 0g,
- Sodium: 54mg,

Cocoa Crusted Grilled Flank Steak

Preparation Time: 15 minutes

Cooking Time: 6 minutes

Servings: 7

Ingredients:

- 1 Tablespoon cocoa powder
- 2 Tablespoon chili powder
- 1 Tablespoon chipotle chili powder
- 1/2 Tablespoon garlic powder
- 1/2 Tablespoon onion powder
- 1-1/2 Tablespoon brown sugar
- 1 Tablespoon cumin
- 1 Tablespoon smoked paprika
- 1 Tablespoon kosher salt
- 1/2 Tablespoon black pepper
- Olive oil
- 4 lb Flank steak

Directions:

1. Whisk together cocoa, chili powder, garlic powder, onion powder, sugar, cumin, paprika, salt, and pepper in a mixing bowl.
2. Drizzle the steak with oil, then rub with the cocoa mixture on both sides.
3. Preheat your wood pellet grill for 15 minutes with the lid closed.
4. Cook the meat on the grill grate for 5 minutes or until the internal temperature reaches 135°F.

5. Remove the meat from the grill and let it cool for 15 minutes to allow the juices to redistribute.
6. Slice the meat against the grain and on a sharp diagonal.

Nutrition:

- Calories 420,
- Total fat 26g,
- Protein 3g,
- Sugar 7g,
- Fiber 8g,
- Sodium: 2410mg

CHAPTER 5:

Pork Recipes

Classic Pulled Pork

Preparation Time: 15 minutes
Cooking Time: 16-20 hours
Servings: 8-12
Ingredients:

- 1 (6- to 8-pound) bone-in pork shoulder
- 2 tablespoons yellow mustard
- 1 batch Not-Just-for-Pork Rub

Directions:

1. Supply your smoker with wood pellets and follow the manufacturer's specific start-up procedure.
2. Coat the pork shoulder all over with mustard and season it with the rub. Place the shoulder on the grill grate and smoke until its internal temperature reaches 195°F.
3. Pull the shoulder from the grill and wrap it completely in aluminum foil or butcher paper. Place it in a cooler, cover the cooler, and let it rest for 1 or 2 hours.
4. Remove the pork shoulder from the cooler and unwrap it. Remove the shoulder bone and pull the pork apart using just your fingers. Serve immediately as desired. Leftovers are encouraged.

Nutrition:

- Calories: 414 Cal Fat: 29 g Carbohydrates: 1 g
- Protein: 38 g Fiber: 0 g

Rub-Injected Pork Shoulder

Preparation Time: 15 minutes

Cooking Time: 16-20 hours

Servings: 8-12

Ingredients:

- 1 (6- to 8-pound) bone-in pork shoulder
- 2 cups Tea Injectable made with Not-Just-for-Pork Rub
- 2 tablespoons yellow mustard
- 1 batch Not-Just-for-Pork Rub

Directions:

1. Supply your smoker with wood pellets and follow the manufacturer's specific start-up procedure.
2. Inject the pork shoulder throughout with the tea injectable.
3. Coat the pork shoulder all over with mustard and season it with the rub.
4. Place the shoulder directly on the grill grate and smoke until its internal temperature reaches 160°F and a dark bark has formed on the exterior. Pull the shoulder from the grill and wrap it completely in aluminum foil or butcher paper.
5. Increase the grill's temperature to 350°F.
6. Return the pork shoulder to the grill and cook until its internal temperature reaches 195°F. Pull the shoulder from the grill and place it in a cooler. Cover the cooler and let the pork rest for 1 or 2 hours.
7. Remove the pork shoulder from the cooler and unwrap it. Remove the shoulder bone and pull the pork apart using just your fingers. Serve immediately.

Nutrition:

- Calories: 257 Cal Fat: 15 g Carbohydrates: 0 g Protein: 29 g
- Fiber: 0 g

Citrus-Brined Pork Roast

Preparation Time: 20 minutes

Cooking Time: 45 minutes

Servings: 6

Ingredients:

- ½ cup salt
- ¼ cup brown sugar
- 3 cloves of garlic, minced
- 2 dried bay leaves
- 6 peppercorns
- 1 lemon, juiced
- ½ teaspoon dried fennel seeds
- ½ teaspoon red pepper flakes
- ½ cup apple juice
- ½ cup orange juice
- 5 pounds pork loin
- 2 tablespoons extra virgin olive oil

Directions:

1. In a bowl, combine the salt, brown sugar, garlic, bay leaves, peppercorns, lemon juice, fennel seeds, pepper flakes, apple juice, and orange juice. Mix to form a paste rub.
2. Rub the mixture on the pork loin and allow to marinate for at least 2 hours in the fridge. Add in the oil.
3. When ready to cook, fire the Traeger Grill to 300F. Use apple wood pellets when cooking. Close the lid and preheat for 15 minutes.

4. Place the seasoned pork loin on the grill grate and close the lid. Cook for 45 minutes. Make sure to flip the pork halfway through the cooking time.

Nutrition:
- Calories: 869;
- Protein: 97.2g;
- Carbs: 15.2g;
- Fat: 43.9g
- Sugar: 13g

Chinese BBQ Pork

Preparation Time: 10 minutes

Cooking Time: 2 hours

Servings: 8

Ingredients:

- 2 pork tenderloins, silver skin removed

For the Marinade:

- ½ teaspoon minced garlic
- 1 1/2 tablespoon brown Sugar
- 1 teaspoon Chinese five-spice
- 1/4 cup honey
- 1 tablespoon Asian sesame oil
- 1/4 cup hoisin sauce
- 2 teaspoons red food coloring
- 1 tablespoon oyster sauce, optional
- 3 tablespoons soy sauce

For the Five-Spice Sauce:

- 1/4 teaspoon Chinese five-spice
- 3 tablespoons brown Sugar
- 1 teaspoon yellow mustard
- 1/4 cup ketchup

Directions:

1. Prepare the marinade and for this, take a small bowl, place all of its ingredients in it and whisk until combined.
2. Take a large plastic bag, pour marinade in it, add pork tenderloin, seal the bag, turn it upside down to coat the pork,

and let it marinate for a minimum of 8 hours in the refrigerator.

3. Switch on the Traeger grill, fill the grill hopper with maple-flavored wood pellets, power the grill on by using the control panel, select 'smoke' on the temperature dial, or set the temperature to 225 degrees F and let it preheat for a minimum of 5 minutes.

4. Meanwhile, remove pork from the marinade, transfer marinade into a small saucepan, place it over medium-high heat and cook for 3 minutes, and then set aside until cooled.

5. When the grill has preheated, open the lid, place pork on the grill grate, shut the grill, and smoke for 2 hours, basting with the marinade halfway.

6. Meanwhile, prepare the five-spice sauce and for this, take a small saucepan, place it over low heat, add all of its ingredients, stir until well combined, and sugar has dissolved and cooked for 5 minutes until hot and thickened, set aside until required.

7. When done, transfer pork to a dish, let rest for 15 minutes, and meanwhile, change the smoking temperature of the grill to 450 degrees F and let it preheat for a minimum of 10 minutes.

8. Then return pork to the grill grate and cook for 3 minutes per side until slightly charred.

9. Transfer pork to a dish, let it rest for 5 minutes, and then serve with prepared five-spice sauce.

Nutrition:

- Calories: 280 Cal
- Fat: 8 g
- Carbs: 12 g
- Protein: 40 g
- Fiber: 0 g

Smoked Sausages

Preparation Time: 15 minutes

Cooking Time: 3 hours

Servings: 4

Ingredients:

- 3 pounds ground pork
- 1 tablespoon onion powder
- 1 tablespoon garlic powder
- 1 teaspoon curing salt
- 4 teaspoon black pepper
- 1/2 tablespoon salt
- 1/2 tablespoon ground mustard
- Hog casings, soaked
- 1/2 cup ice water

Directions:

1. Switch on the Traeger grill, fill the grill hopper with flavored wood pellets, power the grill on by using the control panel, select 'smoke' on the temperature dial, or set the temperature to 225 degrees F and let it preheat for a minimum of 15 minutes.
2. Meanwhile, take a medium bowl, place all the ingredients in it except for water and hog casings, and stir until well mixed.
3. Pour in water, stir until incorporated, place the mixture in a sausage stuffer, then stuff the hog casings and tie the link to the desired length.
4. When the grill has preheated, open the lid, place the sausage links on the grill grate, shut the grill, and smoke for 2 to 3 hours until the internal temperature reaches 155 degrees F.

5. When done, transfer sausages to a dish; let them rest for 5 minutes, then slice and serve.

Nutrition:
- Calories: 230 Cal
- Fat: 22 g
- Carbs: 2 g
- Protein: 14 g
- Fiber: 0 g

Roasted Whole Ham in Apricot Sauce

Preparation Time: 15 minutes

Cooking Time: 2 hours

Servings: 12

Ingredients:

- 8-pound whole ham, bone-in - 16 ounces apricot BBQ sauce
- 2 tablespoon Dijon mustard
- 1/4 cup horseradish

Directions:

1. Switch on the Traeger grill, fill the grill hopper with apple-flavored wood pellets, power the grill on by using the control panel, select 'smoke' on the temperature dial, or set the temperature to 325 degrees F and let it preheat for a minimum of 15 minutes. Meanwhile, take a large roasting pan, line it with foil, and place ham on it.
2. When the grill has preheated, open the lid, place a roasting pan containing ham on the grill grate, shut the grill, and smoke for 1 hour and 30 minutes.
3. Meanwhile, prepare the glaze and for this, take a medium saucepan, place it over medium heat, add BBQ sauce, mustard, and horseradish, stir until mixed and cook for 5 minutes, set aside until required. After 1 hour and 30 minutes of smoking, brush generously with the prepared glaze, and continue smoking for 30 minutes until the internal temperature reaches 135 degrees F.
4. When done, remove the roasting pan from the grill, let rest for 20 minutes, and then cut into slices. Serve ham with remaining glaze.

Nutrition:

- Calories: 157.7 Cal Fat: 5.6 g Carbs: 4.1 g
- Protein: 22.1 g Fiber: 0.1 g

Pork Belly

Preparation Time: 10 minutes

Cooking Time: 3 hours and 30 minutes

Servings: 8

Ingredients:

- 3 pounds pork belly, skin removed
- Pork and poultry rub as needed
- 4 tablespoons salt
- 1/2 teaspoon ground black pepper

Directions:

1. Switch on the Traeger grill, fill the grill hopper with apple-flavored wood pellets, power the grill on by using the control panel, select 'smoke' on the temperature dial, or set the temperature to 275 degrees F and let it preheat for a minimum of 15 minutes.
2. Meanwhile, prepare the pork belly and for this, sprinkle pork and poultry rub, salt, and black pepper on all sides of the pork belly until well coated.
3. When the grill has preheated, open the lid, place the pork belly on the grill grate, and shut the grill, and smoke for 3 hours and 30 minutes until the internal temperature reaches 200 degrees F.
4. When done, transfer pork belly to a cutting board, let it rest for 15 minutes, then cut it into slices and serve.

Nutrition:

- Calories: 430 Cal Fat: 44 g
- Carbs: 1 g Protein: 8 g Fiber: 0 g

Pineapple Pork Barbecue

Preparation Time: 25 minutes

Cooking Time: 60 minutes

Servings: 4

Ingredients:

- 1-pound pork sirloin
- 4 cups pineapple juice
- 3 cloves garlic, minced
- 1 cup carne asada marinade
- 2 tablespoons salt
- 1 teaspoon ground black pepper

Directions:

1. Place all ingredients in a bowl. Massage the pork sirloin to coat with all ingredients. Place inside the fridge to marinate for at least 2 hours.
2. When ready to cook, fire the Traeger Grill to 300F. Use desired wood pellets when cooking the ribs. Close the lid and preheat for 15 minutes.
3. Place the pork sirloin on the grill grate and cook for 45 to 60 minutes. Make sure to flip the pork halfway through the cooking time.
4. At the same time when you put the pork on the grill grate, place the marinade in a pan and place it inside the smoker. Allow the marinade to cook and reduce.
5. Baste the pork sirloin with the reduced marinade before the cooking time ends. Allow to rest before slicing.

Nutrition:

- Calories: 347; Protein: 33.4 g; Carbs: 45.8 g;
- Fat: 4.2g Sugar: 36g

Maple-Smoked Pork Chops

Preparation Time: 10 minutes

Cooking Time: 55 minutes

Servings: 4

Ingredients:

- 4 (8-ounce) pork chops, bone-in or boneless (I use boneless)
- Salt
- Freshly ground black pepper

Directions:

1. Supply your smoker with wood pellets and follow the manufacturer's specific start-up procedure.
2. Drizzle pork chop with salt and pepper to season.
3. Place the chops directly on the grill grate and smoke for 30 minutes.
4. Increase the grill's temperature to 350°F. Continue to cook the chops until their internal temperature reaches 145°F.
5. Remove the pork chops from the grill and let them rest for 5 minutes before serving.

Nutrition:

- Calories: 130 Cal
- Fat: 12 g
- Carbohydrates: 3 g
- Protein: 20 g
- Fiber: 0 g

Apple-Smoked Pork Tenderloin

Preparation Time: 15 minutes

Cooking Time: 4-5 hours

Servings: 4-6

Ingredients:

- 2 (1-pound) pork tenderloins
- 1 batch Not-Just-for-Pork Rub

Directions:

1. Supply your smoker with wood pellets and follow the manufacturer's specific start-up procedure. Preheat the grill.
2. Generously season the tenderloins with the rub.
3. Put tenderloins on the grill and smoke for 4 or 5 hours until their internal temperature reaches 145°F.
4. The tenderloins must be put out of the grill and let them rest for 5-10 minutes, then begin slicing into thin pieces before serving

Nutrition:

- Calories: 180 Cal
- Fat: 8 g
- Carbohydrates: 3 g
- Protein: 24 g
- Fiber: 0 g

Teriyaki Pork Tenderloin

Preparation Time: 30 minutes

Cooking Time: 1 ½ hours to 2 hours

Servings: 4-6

Ingredients:

- 2 (1-pound) pork tenderloins
- 1 batch Easy Teriyaki Marinade
- Smoked salt

Directions:

1. In a large zip-top container, combine the tenderloins and marinade. Seal the bag, turn to coat, and refrigerate the pork for at least 30 minutes—I recommend up to overnight.
2. Supply your smoker with wood pellets and follow the manufacturer's specific start-up procedure. Preheat the grill, with the lid closed, to 180°F.
3. As you get the tenderloins from the marinade, begin seasoning them with smoked salt
4. Place the tenderloins directly on the grill grate and smoke for 1 hour.
5. Increase the grill's temperature to 300°F and continue to cook until the pork's internal temperature reaches 145°F.
6. With the tenderloins removed from the grill, let it cool for at least 5-10 minutes before slicing and serving

Nutrition:

- Calories: 110 Cal
- Fat: 3 g
- Carbohydrates: 2 g
- Protein: 18 g
- Fiber: 0 g

Barbecued Tenderloin

Preparation Time: 5 minutes

Cooking Time: 30 minutes

Servings: 4-6

Ingredients:

- 2 (1-pound) pork tenderloins
- 1 batch Sweet and Spicy Cinnamon Rub

Directions:

1. Supply your smoker with wood pellets and follow the manufacturer's specific start-up procedure. Preheat the grill.
2. Generously season the tenderloins with the rub. Work rub onto meat.
3. Place the tenderloins and smoke internal temperature reaches 145°F.
4. As you put out the tenderloins from the grill, let it cool down for 5-10 minutes before slicing it up and serving it

Nutrition:

- Calories: 186 Cal
- Fat: 4 g
- Carbohydrates: 8 g
- Protein: 29 g
- Fiber:

CHAPTER 6:

Seafood Recipes

Buttered Crab Legs

Preparation Time: 30 minutes

Cooking Time: 10 minutes

Servings: 4

Ingredients:

- 12 tablespoons butter
- 1 tablespoon parsley, chopped
- 1 tablespoon tarragon, chopped
- 1 tablespoon chives, chopped
- 1 tablespoon lemon juice
- 4 lb. king crab legs, split in the center

Directions:

1. Set the Traeger wood pellet grill to 375 degrees F.
2. Preheat it for 15 minutes while the lid is closed.
3. In a pan over medium heat, simmer the butter, herbs, and lemon juice for 2 minutes.
4. Place the crab legs on the grill.
5. Pour half of the sauce on top.
6. Grill for 10 minutes.
7. Serve with the reserved butter sauce.

Serving Suggestion: Garnish with lemon wedges.

Preparation / Cooking Tips: You can also use shrimp for this recipe.

Nutrition:

- Calories: 218
- Protein: 28g
- Carbohydrates: 18g
- Fat: 10g
- Fiber 0g

Grilled Blackened Salmon

Preparation Time: 15 minutes

Cooking Time: 30 minutes

Servings: 4

Ingredients:

- 4 salmon fillet
- Blackened dry rub
- Italian seasoning powder

Directions:

1. Season salmon fillets with a dry rub and seasoning powder.
2. Grill in the Traeger wood pellet grill at 325 degrees F for 10 to 15 minutes per side.

Serving Suggestion: Garnish with lemon wedges.

Preparation / Cooking Tips: You can also drizzle salmon with lemon juice

Nutrition:

- Calories: 258
- Protein: 23g
- Carbohydrates: 20g
- Fat: 12g
- Fiber 0g

BBQ Shrimp

Preparation Time: 20 minutes

Cooking Time: 8 minutes

Servings: 6

Ingredients:

- 2 pound raw shrimp (peeled and deveined)
- ¼ cup extra virgin olive oil
- ½ tsp. paprika
- ½ tsp. red pepper flakes
- 2 garlic cloves (minced)
- 1 tsp. cumin
- 1 lemon (juiced)
- 1 tsp. kosher salt
- 1 tbsp. chili paste
- Bamboo or wooden skewers (soaked for 30 minutes, at least)

Directions:

1. In a large mixing bowl, combine the pepper flakes, cumin, lemon, salt, chili, paprika, garlic, and olive oil. Add the shrimp and toss to combine.
2. Transfer the shrimp and marinade into a zip-lock bag and refrigerate for 4 hours.
3. Take the shrimp off the marinade and allow it to rest until it is a room temperature.
4. Start your grill on smoke, leaving the lid opened for 5 minutes or until the fire starts. Use hickory wood pellet.
5. Cover the lid and l allow the grill to heat to high for 15 minutes.

6. Thread shrimps onto skewers and arrange the skewers on the grill grate.
7. Smoke shrimps for 8 minutes, 4 minutes per side.
8. Serve and enjoy.

Nutrition:
- Calories 267
- Total Fat 11.6g
- Saturated Fat 2g
- Cholesterol 319mg
- Sodium 788mg
- Total Carbohydrate 4.9g
- Dietary Fiber 0.4g
- Total Sugars 1g
- Protein 34.9g
- Calcium 149mg
- Iron 1mg
- Potassium 287mg

Grilled Tuna

Preparation Time: 5 minutes

Cooking Time: 4 minutes

Servings: 4

Ingredients:

- 4 (6 ounce each) tuna steaks (1 inch thick)
- 1 lemon (juiced)
- 1 clove garlic (minced)
- 1 tsp. chili
- 2 tbsp. extra virgin olive oil
- 1 cup white wine
- 3 tbsp. brown sugar
- 1 tsp. rosemary

Directions:

1. In a large mixing bowl, combine the chili, lemon, white wine, sugar, rosemary, olive oil, and garlic. Add the tuna steaks and toss to combine.
2. Transfer the tuna and marinade to a Ziplock bag. Refrigerate for 3 hours.
3. Remove the tuna steaks from the marinade and let them rest for about 1 hour, or until the steaks are at room temperature.
4. Start your grill on smoke, leaving the lid opened for 5 minutes or until the fire starts. Use hickory or mesquite wood pellet.
5. Close the grill lid and let the grill heat on HIGH for 15 minutes.
6. Grease the grill grate with oil and place the tuna on the grill grate. Grill tuna steaks for 4 minutes, 2 minutes per side.

7. Remove the tuna from the grill and let them rest for a few minutes.
8. Serve and enjoy.

Nutrition:
- Calories 455
- Total Fat 17.8g
- Saturated Fat 3.8g
- Cholesterol 84mg
- Sodium 97mg
- Total Carbohydrate 10.2g
- Dietary Fiber 0.6g
- Total Sugars 7.4g
- Protein 51.2g
- Calcium 37mg
- Iron 3mg
- Potassium 648mg

Oyster in Shell

Preparation Time: 25 minutes

Cooking Time: 8 minutes

Servings: 4

Smoke Temperature: 450°F

Ingredients:

- 12 medium oysters
- 1 tsp. oregano
- 1 lemon (juiced)
- 1 tsp. freshly ground black pepper
- 6 tbsp. unsalted butter (melted)
- 1 tsp. salt or more to taste
- 2 garlic cloves (minced)

Garnish:

- 2 ½ tbsp. grated parmesan cheese
- 2 tbsp. freshly chopped parsley

Directions:

1. Start by scrubbing the outside of the shell with a scrub brush under cold running water to remove dirt.
2. Hold an oyster in a towel, flat side up. Insert an oyster knife in the hinge of the oyster.
3. Twist the knife with pressure to pop open the oyster. Run the knife along the oyster hinge to open the shell completely. Discard the top shell.
4. Gently run the knife under the oyster to loosen the oyster foot from the bottom shell.
5. Repeat steps 2 and 3 for the remaining oysters.

6. Combine melted butter, lemon, pepper, salt, garlic, and oregano in a mixing bowl.
7. Pour ½ to 1 tsp. of the butter mixture on each oyster.
8. Start your wood pellet grill on smoke, leaving the lid opened for 5 minutes or until the fire starts.
9. Close the lid and let the grill heat to high with the lid closed for 15 minutes.
10. Gently arrange the oysters onto the grill grate.
11. Grill oyster for 6 to 8 minutes or until the oyster juice is bubbling and the oyster is plump.
12. Remove oysters from heat. Serve and top with grated parmesan and chopped parsley.

Nutrition:

- Calories 200
- Total Fat 19.2g
- Saturated Fat 11.9g
- Cholesterol 66mg
- Sodium 788mg
- Total Carbohydrate 3.9g
- Dietary Fiber 0.8g
- Total Sugars 0.7g
- Protein 4.6g
- Vitamin D 12mcg
- Calcium 93mg
- Iron 2mg
- Potassium 120mg

Grilled King Crab Legs

Preparation Time: 10 minutes

Cooking Time: 25 minutes

Servings: 4

Ingredients:

- 4 pounds king crab legs (split)
- 4 tbsp. lemon juice
- 2 tbsp. garlic powder
- 1 cup butter (melted)
- 2 tsp. brown sugar
- 2 tsp. paprika
- 2 tsp. ground black pepper or more to taste

Directions:

1. In a mixing bowl, combine the lemon juice, butter, sugar, garlic, paprika, and pepper.
2. Arrange the split crab on a baking sheet, split side up.
3. Drizzle ¾ of the butter mixture over the crab legs.
4. Configure your pellet grill for indirect cooking and preheat it to 225°F, using mesquite wood pellets. Arrange the crab legs onto the grill grate, shell side down. Cover the grill and cook for 25 minutes.
5. Remove the crab legs from the grill. Serve and top with the remaining butter mixture.

Nutrition:

- Calories 894 Total Fat 53.2g Saturated Fat 29.3g
- Cholesterol 374mg Sodium 5189mg Total Carbohydrate 6.1g
- Dietary Fiber 1.2g Total Sugars 3gProtein 88.6g
- Vitamin D 32mcg Calcium 301mg Iron 4mg Potassium 119mg

Cajun Smoked Catfish

Preparation Time: 15 minutes

Cooking Time: 2 hours

Servings: 4

Ingredients:

- 4 catfish fillets (5 ounces each)
- ½ cup Cajun seasoning
- 1 tsp. ground black pepper
- 1 tbsp. smoked paprika
- 1/4 tsp. cayenne pepper
- 1 tsp. hot sauce
- 1 tsp. granulated garlic
- 1 tsp. onion powder
- 1 tsp. thyme
- 1 tsp. salt or more to taste
- 2 tbsp. chopped fresh parsley

Directions:

1. Pour water into the bottom of a square or rectangular dish. Add 4 tbsp. salt. Arrange the catfish fillets into the dish. Cover the dish and refrigerate for 3 to 4 hours.
2. Meanwhile, combine the paprika, cayenne, hot sauce, onion, salt, thyme, garlic, pepper, and Cajun seasoning in a mixing bowl.
3. Remove the fish from the dish and let it sit for a few minutes, or until it is at room temperature. Pat the fish fillets dry with a paper towel.
4. Rub the seasoning mixture over each fillet generously.

5. Start your grill on smoke, leaving the lid opened for 5 minutes or until the fire starts.
6. Cover the lid and allow the grill to heat to 200°F, using mesquite hardwood pellets.
7. Arrange the fish fillets onto the grill grate and close the grill. Cook for about 2 hours, or until the fish is flaky.
8. Remove the fillets from the grill and let the fillets rest for a few minutes to cool.
9. Serve and garnish with chopped fresh parsley.

Nutrition:

- Calories 204
- Total Fat 11.1g
- Saturated Fat 2g
- Cholesterol 67mg
- Sodium 991mg
- Total Carbohydrate 2.7g
- Dietary Fiber 1.1g
- Total Sugars 0.6g
- Protein 22.9g
- Calcium 29mg
- Iron 3mg
- Potassium 532mg

Spicy Shrimp

Preparation Time: 45 minutes

Cooking Time: 10 minutes

Servings: 4

Ingredients:

- 3 tablespoons olive oil
- 6 cloves garlic
- 2 tablespoons chicken dry rub
- 6 oz. chili
- 1 1/2 tablespoons white vinegar
- 1 1/2 teaspoons sugar
- 2 lb. shrimp, peeled and deveined

Directions:

1. Add olive oil, garlic, dry rub, chili, vinegar, and sugar in a food processor.
2. Blend until smooth.
3. Transfer mixture to a bowl.
4. Stir in shrimp.
5. Cover and refrigerate for 30 minutes.
6. Preheat the Traeger wood pellet grill to hit for 15 minutes while the lid is closed.
7. Thread shrimp onto skewers.
8. Grill for 3 minutes per side.

Serving Suggestion: Garnish with chopped herbs.

Preparation / Cooking Tips: You can also add vegetables to the skewers.

Nutrition:

- Calories: 250
- Protein: 24g
- Carbohydrates: 18g
- Fat: 13g
- Fiber 0g

Grilled Herbed Tuna

Preparation Time: 4 hours and 15 minutes

Cooking Time: 10 minutes

Servings: 6

Ingredients:

- 6 tuna steaks
- 1 tablespoon lemon zest
- 1 tablespoon fresh thyme, chopped
- 1 tablespoon fresh parsley, chopped
- Garlic salt to taste

Directions:

1. Sprinkle the tuna steaks with lemon zest, herbs, and garlic salt.
2. Cover with foil.
3. Refrigerate for 4 hours.
4. Grill for 3 minutes per side.

Serving Suggestion: Top with lemon slices before serving.

Preparation / Cooking Tips: Take the fish out of the refrigerator 30 minutes before cooking.

Nutrition:

- Calories: 234
- Protein: 25g
- Carbohydrates: 17g
- Fat: 11g
- Fiber 0g

Roasted Snapper

Preparation Time: 30 minutes

Cooking Time: 15 minutes

Servings: 4

Ingredients:

- 4 snapper fillets
- Salt and pepper to taste
- 2 teaspoons dried tarragon
- Olive oil
- 2 lemons, sliced

Directions:

1. Set the Traeger wood pellet grill to high.
2. Preheat it for 15 minutes while the lid is closed.
3. Add 1 fish fillet on top of a foil sheet.
4. Sprinkle with salt, pepper, and tarragon.
5. Drizzle with oil.
6. Place lemon slices on top.
7. Fold and seal the packets.
8. Put the foil packets on the grill.
9. Bake for 15 minutes.
10. Open carefully and serve.

Serving Suggestion: Drizzle with melted butter before serving.

Preparation / Cooking Tips: You can also add asparagus spears or broccoli in the packet to cook with the fish.

Nutrition:

- Calories: 222 Protein: 18g Carbohydrates: 12g Fat: 10g
- Fiber 0g

Fish Fillets with Pesto

Preparation Time: 15 minutes

Cooking Time: 15 minutes

Servings: 6

Ingredients:

- 2 cups fresh basil
- 1 cup parsley, chopped
- 1/2 cup walnuts
- 1/2 cup olive oil
- 1 cup Parmesan cheese, grated
- Salt and pepper to taste
- 4 white fish fillets

Directions:

1. Preheat the Traeger wood pellet grill to high for 15 minutes while the lid is closed.
2. Add all the ingredients except fish to a food processor.
3. Pulse until smooth. Set aside.
4. Season fish with salt and pepper.
5. Grill for 6 to 7 minutes per side.
6. Serve with the pesto sauce.

Serving Suggestion: Garnish with fresh basil leaves.

Preparation / Cooking Tips: You can also spread a little bit of the pesto on the fish before grilling.

Nutrition:

- Calories: 279 Protein: 32g Carbohydrates: 20g
- Fat: 14g Fiber 0g

Halibut with Garlic Pesto

Preparation Time: 20 minutes

Cooking Time: 10 minutes

Servings: 4

Ingredients:

- 4 halibut fillets
- 1 cup olive oil
- Salt and pepper to taste
- 1/4 cup garlic, chopped
- 1/4 cup pine nuts

Directions:

1. Set the Traeger wood pellet grill to smoke.
2. Establish fire for 5 minutes.
3. Set temperature to high.
4. Place a cast iron on a grill.
5. Season fish with salt and pepper.
6. Add fish to the pan.
7. Drizzle with a little oil. Sear for 4 minutes per side.
8. Prepare the garlic pesto by pulsing the remaining ingredients in the food processor until smooth.
9. Serve fish with garlic pesto.

Serving Suggestion: Sprinkle with fresh herbs before serving.

Preparation / Cooking Tips: You can also use other white fish fillets for this recipe.

Nutrition:

- Calories: 298 Protein: 32g Carbohydrates: 20g
- Fat: 16g Fiber 0g

CHAPTER 7:

Vegetarian Recipes

Cajun Style Grilled Corn

Preparation Time: 5 minutes
Cooking Time: 25 minutes
Servings: 4
Ingredients:

- 4 ears corn, with husks

- 1 tsp dried oregano
- 1 tsp paprika
- 1 tsp garlic powder
- 1 tsp onion powder
- 1/2 tsp kosher salt
- 1/2 tsp ground black pepper
- 1/4 tsp dried thyme
- 1/4 tsp cayenne pepper
- 2 tsp butter, melted

Directions:

1. Preheat pellet grill to 375°F.
2. Peel husks back but do not remove. Scrub and remove silks.
3. Mix oregano, paprika, garlic powder, onion powder, salt, pepper, thyme, and cayenne in a small bowl.
4. Brush melted butter over corn.

5. Rub seasoning mixture over each ear of corn. Pull husks up and place corn on grill grates. Grill for about 12-15 minutes, turning occasionally.
6. Remove from grill and allow to cool for about 5 minutes. Remove husks, then serve and enjoy!

Nutrition:
- Calories: 278
- Fat: 17.4 g
- Cholesterol: 40.7 mg
- Carbohydrate: 30.6 g
- Fiber: 4.5 g
- Sugar: 4.6 g
- Protein: 5.4 g

Grilled Cherry Tomato Skewers

Preparation Time: 10 minutes

Cooking Time: 50 minutes

Servings: 4

Ingredients:

- 24 cherry tomatoes
- 1/4 cup olive oil
- 3 tbsp balsamic vinegar
- 4 garlic cloves, minced
- 1 tbsp fresh thyme, finely chopped
- 1 tsp kosher salt
- 1 tsp ground black pepper
- 2 tbsp chives, finely chopped

Directions:

1. Preheat pellet grill to 425°F.
2. In a medium-sized bowl, mix olive oil, balsamic vinegar, garlic, and thyme. Add tomatoes and toss to coat.
3. Let tomatoes sit in the marinade at room temperature for about 30 minutes. Remove tomatoes from marinade and thread 4 tomatoes per skewer.
4. Season both sides of each skewer with kosher salt and ground pepper. Place on grill grate and grill for about 3 minutes on each side, or until each side is slightly charred.
5. Remove from grill and allow to rest for about 5 minutes. Garnish with chives, then serve and enjoy!

Nutrition:

- Calories: 228 Fat: 10 g Cholesterol: 70 mg Carbohydrate: 7 g
- Fiber: 2 g Sugar: 3 g Protein: 27 g

Roasted Vegetable Medley

Preparation Time: 20 minutes

Cooking Time: 50 minutes

Servings: 4 to 6

Ingredients:

- 2 medium potatoes, cut into 1 inch wedges
- 2 red bell peppers, cut into 1 inch cubes
- 1 small butternut squash, peeled and cubed to 1 inch cube
- 1 red onion, cut into 1 inch cubes
- 1 cup broccoli, trimmed
- 2 tbsp olive oil
- 1 tbsp balsamic vinegar
- 1 tbsp fresh rosemary, minced
- 1 tbsp fresh thyme, minced
- 1 tsp kosher salt
- 1 tsp ground black pepper

Directions:

1. Preheat pellet grill to 425°F.
2. In a large bowl, combine potatoes, peppers, squash, and onion.
3. In a small bowl, whisk together olive oil, balsamic vinegar, rosemary, thyme, salt, and pepper.
4. Pour marinade over vegetables and toss to coat. Allow resting for about 15 minutes.
5. Place marinated vegetables into a grill basket, and place a grill basket on the grill grate. Cook for about 30-40 minutes, occasionally tossing in the grill basket.

6. Remove veggies from grill and transfer to a serving dish. Allow to cool for 5 minutes, then serve and enjoy!

Nutrition:
- Calories: 158.6
- Fat: 7.4 g
- Cholesterol: 0
- Carbohydrate: 22 g
- Fiber: 7.2 g
- Sugar: 3.1 g
- Protein: 5.2 g

Grilled Corn with Honey Butter

Preparation Time: 15 minutes

Cooking Time: 10 minutes

Servings: 6

Ingredients:

- 6 pieces corn, husked
- 2 tablespoons olive oil
- Salt and pepper to taste
- ½ cup butter, room temperature
- ½ cup honey

Directions:

1. Fire the Traeger Grill to 350F. Use desired wood pellets when cooking. Keep lid unopened to preheat until 15 minutes
2. Coat corn with oil and add salt and pepper
3. Place the corn on the grill grate and cook for 10 minutes. Make sure to flip the corn halfway through the cooking time for even cooking.
4. Meanwhile, mix the butter and honey in a small bowl. Set aside.
5. Remove corn from grill and coat with honey butter sauce

Nutrition:

- Calories: 387 Cal
- Fat: 21.6 g
- Carbohydrates: 51.2 g
- Protein: 5 g
- Fiber: 0 g

Smoked Mushrooms

Preparation Time: 20 minutes

Cooking Time: 2 hours

Servings: 6

Ingredients:

- 6-12 large Portobello mushrooms
- Sea salt
- black pepper
- Extra virgin olive oil
- Herbs de Provence

Directions:

1. Preheat the smoker to 200°F while adding water and wood chips to the smoker bowl and tray, respectively.
2. Wash and dry mushrooms
3. Rub the mushrooms with olive oil, salt and pepper seasoning with herbs in a bowl.
4. Place the mushrooms with the cap side down on the smoker rack. Smoke the mushrooms for 2 hours while adding water and wood chips to the smoker after every 60 minutes.
5. Remove the mushrooms and serve

Nutrition:

- Calories: 106 Cal
- Fat: 6 g
- Carbohydrates: 5 g
- Protein: 8 g
- Fiber: 0.9 g

Smoked Cherry Tomatoes

Preparation Time: 20 minutes

Cooking Time: 1 ½ hours

Servings: 8-10

Ingredients:

- 2 pints of tomatoes

Directions:

1. Preheat the electric smoker to 225°F while adding wood chips and water to the smoker.
2. Clean the tomatoes with clean water and dry them off properly.
3. Place the tomatoes on the pan and place the pan in the smoker.
4. Smoke for 90 minutes while adding water and wood chips to the smoker.

Nutrition:

- Calories: 16 Cal
- Fat: 0 g
- Carbohydrates: 3 g
- Protein: 1 g
- Fiber: 1 g

Smoked and Smashed New Potatoes

Preparation Time: 5 minutes

Cooking Time: 8 hours

Servings: 4

Ingredients:

- 1-1/2 pounds small new red potatoes or fingerlings
- Extra virgin olive oil
- Sea salt and black pepper
- 2 tbsp softened butter

Directions:

1. Let the potatoes dry. Once dried, put in a pan and coat with salt, pepper, and extra virgin olive oil.
2. Place the potatoes on the topmost rack of the smoker.
3. Smoke for 60 minutes.
4. Once done, take them out and smash each one
5. Mix with butter and season

Nutrition:

- Calories: 258 Cal
- Fat: 2.0 g
- Carbohydrates: 15.5 g
- Protein: 4.1 g
- Fiber: 1.5 g

Smoked Brussels Sprouts

Preparation Time: 15 minutes

Cooking Time: 45 minutes

Servings: 6

Ingredients:

- 1-1/2 pounds Brussels sprouts
- 2 cloves of garlic minced
- 2 tbsp extra virgin olive oil
- Sea salt and cracked black pepper

Directions:

1. Rinse sprouts
2. Remove the outer leaves and brown bottoms off the sprouts.
3. Place sprouts in a large bowl, then coat with olive oil.
4. Add a coat of garlic, salt, and pepper and transfer them to the pan.
5. Add to the top rack of the smoker with water and woodchips.
6. Smoke for 45 minutes or until reaches 250°F temperature.
7. Serve

Nutrition:

- Calories: 84 Cal
- Fat: 4.9 g
- Carbohydrates: 7.2 g
- Protein: 2.6 g
- Fiber: 2.9 g

Apple Veggie Burger

Preparation Time: 10 minutes

Cooking Time: 35 minutes

Servings: 6

Ingredients:

- 3 tbsp ground flax or ground chia
- 1/3 cup of warm water
- 1/2 cups rolled oats
- 1 cup chickpeas, drained and rinsed
- 1 tsp cumin
- 1/2 cup onion
- 1 tsp dried basil
- 2 granny smith apples
- 1/3 cup parsley or cilantro, chopped
- 2 tbsp soy sauce
- 2 tsp liquid smoke
- 2 cloves garlic, minced
- 1 tsp chili powder
- 1/4 tsp black pepper

Directions:

1. Preheat the smoker to 225°F while adding wood chips and water to it.
2. In a separate bowl, add chickpeas and mash. Mix together the remaining ingredients along with the dipped flax seeds.
3. Form patties from this mixture.

4. Put the patties on the rack of the smoker and smoke them for 20 minutes on each side.
5. When brown, take them out and serve.

Nutrition:
- Calories: 241 Cal
- Fat: 5 g
- Carbohydrates: 40 g
- Protein: 9 g
- Fiber: 10.3 g

Smokey Roasted Cauliflower

Preparation Time: 10 minutes

Cooking Time: 1 hour 20 minutes

Servings: 4 to 6

Ingredients:

- 1 head cauliflower
- 1 cup parmesan cheese

Spice ingredients:

- 1 tbsp olive oil - 2 cloves garlic, chopped
- 1 tsp kosher salt
- 1 tsp smoked paprika

Directions:

1. Preheat pellet grill to 180°F. If applicable, set the smoke setting to high.
2. Cut cauliflower into bite-size flowerets and place in a grill basket. Place basket on the grill grate and smoke for an hour.
3. Mix spice ingredients in a small bowl while the cauliflower is smoking. Remove cauliflower from the grill after an hour and let cool. Change grill temperature to 425°F. After the cauliflower has cooled, put cauliflower in a resealable bag, and pour marinade in the bag. Toss to combine in the bag.
4. Place cauliflower back in a grill basket and return to grill. Roast in the grill basket for 10-12 minutes or until the outsides begin to get crispy and golden brown.
5. Remove from grill and transfer to a serving dish. Sprinkle parmesan cheese over the cauliflower and rest for a few minutes so the cheese can melt. Serve and enjoy!

Nutrition:

- Calories: 70 Fat: 35 g Cholesterol: 0 Carbohydrate: 7 g
- Fiber: 3 g Sugar: 3 g Protein: 3 g

Crispy Maple Bacon Brussels Sprouts

Preparation Time: 15 minutes

Cooking Time: 1 hour

Servings: 6

Ingredients:

- 1 lb brussels sprouts, trimmed and quartered
- 6 slices thick-cut bacon
- 3 tbsp maple syrup
- 1 tsp olive oil
- 1/2 tsp kosher salt
- 1/2 tsp ground black pepper

Directions:

1. Preheat pellet grill to 425°F.
2. Cut bacon into 1/2 inch thick slices.
3. Place brussels sprouts in a single layer in the cast iron skillet. Drizzle with olive oil and maple syrup, then toss to coat. Sprinkle bacon slices on top, then season with kosher salt and black pepper.
4. Place skillet in the pellet grill and roast for about 40 to 45 minutes, or until the brussels sprouts are caramelized and brown.
5. Remove skillet from grill and allow brussels sprouts to cool for about 5 to 10 minutes. Serve and enjoy!

Nutrition:

- Calories: 175.3 Fat: 12.1 g Cholesterol: 6.6 mg
- Carbohydrate: 13.6 g Fiber: 2.9 g
- Sugar: 7.6 g Protein: 4.8 g

Sweet Jalapeño Cornbread

Preparation Time: 20 minutes

Cooking Time: 50 minutes

Servings: 12

Ingredients:

- 2/3 cup margarine, softened
- 2/3 cup white sugar
- 2 cups cornmeal
- 1 1/3 cups all-purpose flour
- 4 tsp baking powder
- 1 tsp kosher salt
- 3 eggs
- 1 2/3 cups milk
- 1 cup jalapeños, deseeded and chopped
- Butter, to line baking dish

Directions:

1. Preheat pellet grill to 400°F.
2. Beat margarine and sugar together in a medium-sized bowl until smooth.
3. In another bowl, combine cornmeal, flour, baking powder, and salt.
4. In a third bowl, combine and whisk eggs and milk.
5. Pour 1/3 of the milk mixture and 1/3 of the flour mixture into the margarine mixture at a time, whisking just until mixed after each pour.
6. Once thoroughly combined, stir in chopped jalapeño.
7. Lightly butter the bottom of the baking dish. Pour the cornbread mixture evenly into the baking dish.

8. Place dish on grill grates and close the lid. Cook for about 23-25 minutes, or until thoroughly cooked. The way to test is by inserting a toothpick into the center of the cornbread - it should come out clean once removed.
9. Remove the dish from the grill and allow to rest for 10 minutes before slicing and serving.

Nutrition:
- Calories: 160
- Fat: 6 g
- Cholesterol: 15 mg
- Carbohydrate: 25 g
- Fiber: 10 g
- Sugar: 0.5 g
- Protein: 3 g

Broccoli with Lemon and Pepper

Preparation Time: 15 minutes

Cooking Time: 3 Minutes

Servings: 1-2

Ingredients:

- 2 cups of broccoli, fresh
- 1 tablespoon of canola oil
- 1 teaspoon of lemon pepper

Directions:

1. Place the grill; grate inside the unit, and close the hood.
2. Preheat the grill by turning at high for 10 minutes.
3. Meanwhile, mix broccoli with lemon pepper and canola oil.
4. Toss well to coat the ingredients thoroughly.
5. Place it on a grill grade once add food appears.
6. Lock the unit and cook for 3 minutes at medium.
7. Take out and serve.

Nutrition:

- Calories: 96
- Total Fat: 7.3g
- Saturated Fat: 0.5g
- Cholesterol: 0mg
- Sodium: 30mg
- Total Carbohydrate: 6.7g
- Dietary Fiber 2.7g
- Total Sugars: 1.6g
- Protein: 2.7g

CHAPTER 8:

Vegan Recipes

Roasted Cauliflower

Preparation Time: 15 minutes

Cooking Time: 10 minutes

Servings: 4 to 6

Ingredients:

- 1 Cauliflower head, cut into florets
- 1 tbsp. Oil
- 1 cup grated Parmesan
- 2 Garlic cloves, cursed
- ½ Tsp. Black pepper

- ½ tsp. of Salt
- ¼ tsp. of Paprika

Directions:

1. Let the grill heat to 180F with the lid closed.
2. Place the cauliflower florets on the grill. Smoke for 1 hour. In the meantime, combine the remaining ingredients but not the cheese. Once done, remove the florets.
3. Increase the heat to 450F. Once heated, brush the florets with the mixture. Place on a cooking tray and on the grill. Roast for 10 minutes.
4. Sprinkle with cheese and let it sit on the grill with the lid closed until melted
5. Serve as it is or as a side dish. Enjoy!

Nutrition:

- Calories: 45
- Protein: 7g
- Carbs: 7g
- Fat: 2g

Roasted Asparagus

Preparation Time: 5 minutes

Cooking Time: 30 minutes

Servings: 4 to 6

Ingredients:

- 1 bunch of Asparagus
- Salmon seasoning as needed
- 2 tbsp. Oil, or as needed

Directions:

1. Season the asparagus with salmon seasoning and drizzle with oil. Make sure to coat well.
2. Let the grill heat to 350F with the lid closed.
3. Grill the asparagus for 30 minutes.
4. Serve and enjoy!

Nutrition:

- Calories: 70g
- Protein: 4g
- Carbs: 7g
- Fat: 4g

Grilled Mixed Veggies

Preparation Time: 15 minutes

Cooking Time: 20 minutes

Servings: 4 to 6

Smoke Temperature: 450°F

Ingredients:

- 1 Tomato, Large
- 1 Squash
- 1 Zucchini
- 1 Onion, red
- 1 Potato, Sweet
- Black pepper and Salt to taste
- Oil

Directions:

1. Let the grill heat with closed lit to high.
2. Slice the veggies into slices (1/4 inch).
3. Brush each slice with oil. Season with black pepper and salt.
4. First grill the squash, zucchini, onion, and sweet potato for 20min. turn them halfway.
5. Add the tomato slices 5 minutes before the cooking is done.
6. Serve them with your main dish and enjoy!

Nutrition:

- Calories: 105
- Protein: 5g
- Carbs: 23g
- Fat: 8g

Grilled Corn

Preparation Time: 15 minutes

Cooking Time: 25 minutes

Servings: 6

Smoke Temperature: 450°F

Ingredients:

- 6 fresh ears corn
- Salt
- Black pepper
- Olive oil
- Vegetable seasoning
- Butter for serving

Directions:

1. Let the grill heat to high with the lid closed.
2. Peel the husks. Remove the corn's silk. Rub with black pepper, salt, vegetable seasoning, and oil.
3. Close the husks and grill for 25 minutes. Turn them occasionally.
4. Serve topped with butter, and enjoy!

Nutrition:

- Calories: 70
- Protein: 3g
- Carbs: 18g
- Fat: 2g

Thyme - Rosemary Mash Potatoes

Preparation Time: 20 minutes

Cooking Time: 1 hour

Servings: 6

Smoke Temperature: 350°F

Ingredients:

- 4 ½ lbs. Potatoes, russet
- Salt
- 1 pint of Heavy cream
- 3 Thyme sprigs + 2 tbsp. for garnish
- 2 Rosemary sprigs
- 6 - 7 Sage leaves
- 6 - 7 Black peppercorns
- Black pepper to taste
- 2 stick Butter, softened
- 2 Garlic cloves, chopped

Directions:

1. Let the grill heat to 350F with the lid closed.
2. Peel the russet potatoes. Cut into small pieces and place them in a baking dish. Fill it with water (1 ½ cups). Place on the grill and cook with the lid closed for about 1 hour.
3. In the meantime, combine garlic, peppercorns, herbs and cream in a saucepan. Place on the grate and cook covered for about 15 minutes. Once done, strain to remove the garlic and herbs. Keep warm.
4. Drain the potatoes and place them in a stockpot. Rice them with a fork and pour 2/3 of the mixture.

5. Add 1 stick softened butter and salt. Add more cream to get the desired consistency.

6. Serve right away.

Nutrition:

- Calories: 180
- Protein: 4g
- Carbs: 28g
- Fat: 10g

Grilled Broccoli

Preparation Time: 15 minutes

Cooking Time: 10 minutes

Servings: 4 to 6

Smoke Temperature: 450°F

Ingredients:

- 4 bunches of Broccoli
- 4 tbsp. Olive oil
- Black pepper and salt to taste
- ½ Lemon, the juice
- ½ Lemon cut into wedges

Directions:

1. Let the grill heat to High with the lid closed.
2. In a bowl add the broccoli and drizzle with oil. Coat well. Season with salt.
3. Grill for 5 minutes and then flip. Cook for 3 minutes more.
4. Once done, transfer on a plate. Squeeze lemon on top and serve with lemon wedges. Enjoy!

Nutrition:

- Calories: 35g
- Protein: 2.5g
- Carbs: 5g
- Fat: 1g

Smoked Coleslaw

Preparation Time: 15 minutes

Cooking Time: 25 minutes

Servings: 8 to 12

Smoke Temperature: 180°F

Ingredients:

- 1 shredded Purple Cabbage
- 1 shredded Green Cabbage
- 2 Scallions, sliced
- 1 cup Carrots, shredded
- 1 tbsp. of Celery Seed
- 1/8 cup of White vinegar
- 1 ½ cups Mayo
- Black pepper and salt to taste

Directions:

1. Let the grill heat to 180F with the lid closed.
2. On a tray, spread the carrots and cabbage. Place the tray on the grate and smoke for about 25 minutes.
3. Transfer to the fridge to cool.
4. In the meantime, make the dressing. In a bowl combine the ingredients. Mix well.
5. Transfer the veggies to a bowl. Drizzle with the sauce and toss
6. Serve sprinkled with scallions. You can serve it as a side dish or as a salad. Enjoy!

Nutrition:

- Calories: 35g Protein: 1g Carbs: 5g Fat: 5g

The Best Potato Roast

Preparation Time: 15 minutes

Cooking Time: 35 minutes

Servings: 6

Smoke Temperature: 450°F

Ingredients:

- 4 Potatoes, large (scrubbed)
- 2 tbsp. Vegetable oil
- 1 ½ cups gravy (beef or chicken)
- Rib seasoning to taste
- 1 ½ cups Cheddar cheese
- Black pepper and salt to taste
- 2 tbsp. sliced Scallions

Directions:

1. Let the grill heat to high with the lid closed.
2. Slice each potato into wedges or fries. Transfer into a bowl and drizzle with oil. Season with Rib seasoning.
3. Spread the wedges/fries on a baking sheet (rimmed). Roast for about 20 minutes. Turn the wedges/fries and cook for 15 minutes more.
4. In the meantime, warm the chicken/beef gravy in a saucepan. Cut the cheese into small cubes.
5. Once done cooking, place the potatoes on a plate or into a bowl. Distribute the cut cheese and pour hot gravy on top.
6. Serve garnished with scallion. Season with pepper. Enjoy!

Nutrition:

- Calories: 220 Protein: 3g Carbs: 38g Fat: 15g

CHAPTER 9:

Poultry Recipes

Traeger Chile Lime Chicken

Preparation Time: 12 minutes

Cooking Time: 15 minutes

Servings: 1

Ingredients:

- 1 chicken breast
- 1 Tablespoon oil
- 1 Tablespoon spiceology Chile Lime Seasoning

Directions:

1. Preheat your Traeger to 400F.
2. Brush the chicken breast with oil, then sprinkle the chile-lime seasoning and salt.
3. Place the chicken breast on the grill and cook for 7 minutes on each side or until the internal temperature reaches 165F.
4. Serve when hot and enjoy.

Nutrition:

- Calories 131,
- Total fat 5g,
- Protein 19g,
- Fiber 1g,
- Sodium 235mg

Traeger Sheet Pan Chicken Fajitas

Preparation Time: 10 minutes

Cooking Time: 10 minutes

Servings: 10

Ingredients:

- 2 lb chicken breast
- 1 onion, sliced
- 1 red bell pepper, seeded and sliced
- 1 orange-red bell pepper, seeded and sliced
- 1 Tablespoon salt
- 1/2 Tablespoon onion powder
- 1/2 Tablespoon granulated garlic
- 2 Tablespoon Spiceologist Chile Margarita Seasoning
- 2 Tablespoon oil

Directions:

1. Preheat the Traeger to 450F and line a baking sheet with parchment paper.
2. In a mixing bowl, combine seasonings and oil, then toss with the peppers and chicken.
3. Place the baking sheet in the Traeger and let heat for 10 minutes with the lid closed.
4. Open the lid and place the veggies and the chicken in a single layer. Close the lid and cook for 10 minutes or until the chicken is no longer pink.
5. Serve with warm tortillas and top with your favorite toppings.

Nutrition:

- Calories 211, Total fat 6g, Protein 29g, Fiber 1g,
- Sodium 360mg

Traeger Asian Miso Chicken Wings

Preparation Time: 15 minutes

Cooking Time: 25 minutes

Servings: 6

Ingredients:

- 2 lb chicken wings
- 3/4 cup soy
- 1/2 cup pineapple juice
- 1 Tablespoon sriracha
- 1/8 cup miso
- 1/8 cup gochujang
- 1/2 cup water
- 1/2 cup oil
- Togarashi

Directions:

1. Preheat the Traeger to 375F
2. Combine all the ingredients except togarashi in a zip lock bag. Toss until the chicken wings are well coated. Refrigerate for 12 hours
3. Pace the wings on the grill grates and close the lid. Cook for 25 minutes or until the internal temperature reaches 165F
4. Remove the wings from the Traeger and sprinkle Togarashi.

Nutrition:

- Calories 703, Total fat 56g, Protein 27g,
- Fiber 1g, Sodium 1156mg

Smoked Turkey Mayo with Green Apple

Preparation Time: 20 minutes

Cooking Time: 4 hours 10 minutes

Servings: 10

Ingredients:

- Whole turkey (4-lbs., 1.8-kg.)

The Rub

- Mayonnaise – ½ cup
- Salt – ¾ teaspoon
- Brown sugar – ¼ cup
- Ground mustard – 2 tablespoons
- Black pepper – 1 teaspoon
- Onion powder – 1 ½ tablespoons
- Ground cumin – 1 ½ tablespoons
- Chili powder – 2 tablespoons
- Cayenne pepper – ½ tablespoon
- Old Bay Seasoning – ½ teaspoon

The Filling

- Sliced green apples – 3 cups

Directions:

1. Place salt, brown sugar, brown mustard, black pepper, onion powder, ground cumin, chili powder, cayenne pepper, and old bay seasoning in a bowl, then mix well. Set aside.
2. Next, fill the turkey cavity with sliced green apples, then baste mayonnaise over the turkey skin.
3. Sprinkle the dry spice mixture over the turkey, then wrap with aluminum foil.

4. Marinate the turkey for at least 4 hours or overnight and store it in the fridge to keep it fresh.
5. On the next day, remove the turkey from the fridge and thaw at room temperature.
6. Meanwhile, plug the wood pellet smoker, then fill the hopper with the wood pellet. Turn the switch on.
7. Set the wood pellet smoker for indirect heat then adjust the temperature to 275°F (135°C).
8. Unwrap the turkey and place it in the wood pellet smoker.
9. Smoke the turkey for 4 hours or until the internal temperature has reached 170°F (77°C).
10. Remove the smoked turkey from the wood pellet smoker and serve.

Nutrition:

- Calories: 340
- Carbs: 40g
- Fat: 10g
- Protein: 21g

Buttery Smoked Turkey Beer

Preparation Time: 15 minutes

Cooking Time: 4 hours

Servings: 6

Ingredients:

- Whole turkey (4-lbs., 1.8-kg.)

The Brine

- Beer – 2 cans
- Salt – 1 tablespoon
- White sugar – 2 tablespoons
- Soy sauce – ¼ cup
- Cold water – 1 quart

The Rub

- Unsalted butter – 3 tablespoons
- Smoked paprika – 1 teaspoon
- Garlic powder – 1 ½ teaspoon
- Pepper – 1 teaspoon
- Cayenne pepper – ¼ teaspoon

Directions:

1. Pour beer into a container, then add salt, white sugar, and soy sauce, then stir well.
2. Put the turkey into the brine mixture cold water over the turkey. Make sure that the turkey is completely soaked.
3. Soak the turkey in the brine for at least 6 hours or overnight and store in the fridge to keep it fresh.
4. On the next day, remove the turkey from the fridge and take it out of the brine mixture.

5. Wash and rinse the turkey, then pat it dry.
6. Next, plug the wood pellet smoker, then fill the hopper with the wood pellet. Turn the switch on.
7. Set the wood pellet smoker for indirect heat, then adjust the temperature to 275°F (135°C).
8. Open the beer can, then push it in the turkey cavity.
9. Place the seasoned turkey in the wood pellet smoker and make a tripod using the beer can and the two turkey-legs.
10. Smoke the turkey for 4 hours or until the internal temperature has reached 170°F (77°C).
11. Once it is done, remove the smoked turkey from the wood pellet smoker and transfer it to a serving dish.

Nutrition:

- Calories: 229
- Carbs: 34g
- Fat: 8g
- Protein: 3g

Barbecue Chili Smoked Turkey Breast

Preparation Time: 15 minutes

Cooking Time: 4 hours 20 minutes

Servings: 8

Ingredients:

- Turkey breast (3-lb., 1.4-kg.)

The Rub

- Salt – ¾ teaspoon
- Pepper – ½ teaspoon

The Glaze

- Olive oil – 1 tablespoon
- Ketchup – ¾ cup
- White vinegar – 3 tablespoons
- Brown sugar – 3 tablespoons
- Smoked paprika – 1 tablespoon
- Chili powder – ¾ teaspoon
- Cayenne powder – ¼ teaspoon

Directions:

1. Score the turkey breast at several places, then sprinkle salt and pepper over it.
2. Let the seasoned turkey breast rest for approximately 10 minutes.
3. In the meantime, plug the wood pellet smoker, then fill the hopper with the wood pellet. Turn the switch on.
4. Set the wood pellet smoker for indirect heat, then adjust the temperature to 275°F (135°C).
5. Place the seasoned turkey breast in the wood pellet smoker and smoke for 2 hours.

6. In the meantime, combine olive oil, ketchup, white vinegar, brown sugar, smoked paprika, chili powder, garlic powder, and cayenne pepper in a saucepan, then stir until incorporated. Wait to simmer, then remove from heat.
7. After 2 hours of smoking, baste the sauce over the turkey breast and continue smoking for another 2 hours.
8. Once the internal temperature of the smoked turkey breast has reached 170°F (77°C), remove from the wood pellet smoker and wrap with aluminum foil.
9. Let the smoked turkey breast rest for approximately 15 minutes to 30 minutes, then unwrap it.
10. Cut the smoked turkey breast into thick slices, then serve.

Nutrition:

- Calories: 290
- Carbs: 2g
- Fat: 3g
- Protein: 63g

Apple wood-Smoked Whole Turkey

Preparation Time: 10 minutes

Cooking Time: 5 hours

Servings: 6

Ingredients:

- 1 (10- to 12-pound) turkey, giblets removed
- Extra-virgin olive oil for rubbing
- ¼ cup poultry seasoning
- 8 tablespoons (1 stick) unsalted butter, melted
- ½ cup apple juice
- 2 teaspoons dried sage
- 2 teaspoons dried thyme

Directions:

1. Supply your smoker with wood pellets and follow the manufacturer's specific start-up procedure. Preheat, with the lid closed, to 250°F.
2. Rub the turkey with oil and season with the poultry seasoning inside and out, getting under the skin.
3. In a bowl, combine the melted butter, apple juice, sage, and thyme to use for basting.
4. Put the turkey in a roasting pan, place on the grill, close the lid, and grill for 5 to 6 hours, basting every hour until the skin is brown and crispy, or until a meat thermometer inserted in the thickest part of the thigh reads 165°F.
5. Let the turkey meat rest for about 15 to 20 minutes before carving.

Nutrition:

- Calories: 180 Carbs: 3g Fat: 2g Protein: 39g

Buffalo Chicken Thighs

Preparation Time: 30 minutes

Cooking Time: 6 Hours

Servings: 1

Ingredients:

- 4-6 skinless, boneless chicken thighs
- Traeger Pork and poultry rub
- 4 tablespoons of butter
- 1 cup of sauce; buffalo wing
- Bleu cheese crumbles
- Ranch dressing

Directions:

1. Set the grill to preheat by keeping the temperature to 450 degrees F and keeping the lid closed
2. Now season the chicken thighs with the poultry rub and then place it on the grill grate
3. Cook it for 8 to 10 minutes while making sure to flip it once midway
4. Now take a small saucepan and cook the wing sauce along with butter by keeping the flame on medium heat. Make sure to stir in between to avoid lumps
5. Now take the cooked chicken and dip it into the wing sauce and the butter mix. Make sure to coat both the sides in an even manner
6. Take the chicken thighs that have been sauced to the grill and then cook for further 15 minutes. Do so until the internal temperature reads 175 degrees

7. Sprinkle bleu cheese and drizzle the ranch dressing
8. Serve and enjoy

Nutrition:
- Carbohydrates: 29 g
- Protein: 19 g
- Sodium: 25 mg
- Cholesterol: 19 mg

Savory-Sweet Turkey Legs

Preparation Time: 10 minutes

Cooking Time: 5 hours

Servings: 4

Ingredients:

- 1 gallon hot water
- 1 cup curing salt (such as Morton Tender Quick)
- ¼ cup packed light brown sugar
- 1 teaspoon freshly ground black pepper
- 1 teaspoon ground cloves
- 1 bay leaf
- 2 teaspoons liquid smoke
- 4 turkey legs
- Mandarin Glaze, for serving

Directions:

1. In a huge container with a lid, stir together the water, curing salt, brown sugar, pepper, cloves, bay leaf, and liquid smoke until the salt and sugar are dissolved; let come to room temperature.
2. Submerge the turkey legs in the seasoned brine, cover, and refrigerate overnight.
3. When ready to smoke, remove the turkey legs from the brine and rinse them; discard the brine.
4. Supply your smoker with wood pellets and follow the manufacturer's specific start-up procedure. Preheat, with the lid closed, to 225°F.

5. Arrange the turkey legs on the grill, close the lid, and smoke for 4 to 5 hours, or until dark brown and a meat thermometer inserted in the thickest part of the meat reads 165°F.
6. Serve with Mandarin Glaze on the side or drizzled over the turkey legs.

Nutrition:

- Calories: 190
- Carbs: 1g
- Fat: 9g
- Protein: 24g

Lemon Chicken Breast

Preparation Time: 15 minutes

Cooking Time: 30 minutes

Servings: 4

Ingredients:

- 6 chicken breasts, skinless and boneless
- ½ cup oil
- 1-3 fresh thyme sprigs
- 1 teaspoon ground black pepper
- 2 teaspoon salt
- 2 teaspoons honey
- 1 garlic clove, chopped
- 1 lemon, juiced and zested
- Lemon wedges

Directions:

1. Take a bowl and prepare the marinade by mixing thyme, pepper, salt, honey, garlic, lemon zest, and juice. Mix well until dissolved
2. Add oil and whisk
3. Clean breasts and pat them dry, place in a bag alongside marinade, and let them sit in the fridge for 4 hours
4. Preheat your smoker to 400 degrees F
5. Drain chicken and smoke until the internal temperature reaches 165 degrees, for about 15 minutes

Nutrition:

- Calories: 230 Fats: 7g Carbs: 1g Fiber: 2g

Maple and Bacon Chicken

Preparation Time: 20 minutes

Cooking Time: 1 and ½ hours

Servings: 7

Ingredients:

- 4 boneless and skinless chicken breast
- Salt as needed
- Fresh pepper
- 12 slices bacon, uncooked
- 1 cup maple syrup
- ½ cup melted butter
- 1 teaspoon liquid smoke

Directions:

1. Preheat your smoker to 250 degrees Fahrenheit
2. Season the chicken with pepper and salt
3. Wrap the breast with 3 bacon slices and cover the entire surface
4. Secure the bacon with toothpicks
5. Take a medium-sized bowl and stir in maple syrup, butter, liquid smoke, and mix well
6. Reserve 1/3rd of this mixture for later use
7. Submerge the chicken breast into the butter mix and coat them well
8. Place a pan in your smoker and transfer the chicken to your smoker
9. Smoker for 1 to 1 and a ½ hours

10. Brush the chicken with reserved butter and smoke for 30 minutes more until the internal temperature reaches 165 degrees Fahrenheit

Nutrition:
- Calories: 458
- Fats: 20g
- Carbs: 65g
- Fiber: 1g

Paprika Chicken

Preparation Time: 20 minutes

Cooking Time: 2 – 4 hours

Servings: 7

Ingredients:

- 4-6 chicken breast
- 4 tablespoons olive oil
- 2 tablespoons smoked paprika
- ½ tablespoon salt
- ¼ teaspoon pepper
- 2 teaspoons garlic powder
- 2 teaspoons garlic salt
- 2 teaspoons pepper
- 1 teaspoon cayenne pepper
- 1 teaspoon rosemary

Directions:

1. Preheat your smoker to 220 degrees Fahrenheit using your favorite wood Pellets
2. Prepare your chicken breast according to your desired shapes and transfer to a greased baking dish
3. Take a medium bowl and add spices, stir well
4. Press the spice mix over the chicken and transfer the chicken to the smoker
5. Smoke for 1-1 and a ½ hours
6. Turn-over and cook for 30 minutes more
7. Once the internal temperature reaches 165 degrees Fahrenheit

8. Remove from the smoker and cover with foil
9. Allow it to rest for 15 minutes

Nutrition:
- Calories: 237
- Fats: 6.1g
- Carbs: 14g
- Fiber: 3g

Sweet Sriracha Barbecue Chicken

Preparation Time: 30 minutes

Cooking Time: 1 and ½-2 hours

Servings: 5

Ingredients:

- 1 cup sriracha
- ½ cup butter
- ½ cup molasses
- ½ cup ketchup
- ¼ cup firmly packed brown sugar
- 1 teaspoon salt
- 1 teaspoon fresh ground black pepper
- 1 whole chicken, cut into pieces
- ½ teaspoon fresh parsley leaves, chopped

Directions:

1. Preheat your smoker to 250 degrees Fahrenheit using cherry wood
2. Take a medium saucepan and place it over low heat, stir in butter, sriracha, ketchup, molasses, brown sugar, mustard, pepper, and salt and keep stirring until the sugar and salt dissolves
3. Divide the sauce into two portions
4. Brush the chicken half with the sauce and reserve the remaining for serving
5. Make sure to keep the sauce for serving on the side and keep the other portion for basting

6. Transfer chicken to your smoker rack and smoke for about 1 and a ½ to 2 hours until the internal temperature reaches 165 degrees Fahrenheit
7. Sprinkle chicken with parsley and serve with reserved Barbecue sauce

Nutrition:

- Calories: 148
- Fats: 0.6g
- Carbs: 10g
- Fiber: 1g

CHAPTER 10:

Extra Recipes

Beer Mopping Sauce
Preparation Time: 5 minutes
Cooking Time: 20 minutes
Servings: 8 to 12 **Ingredients:**

- 12 ounces of beer
- ½ cup water
- ½ cup cider vinegar
- ½ cup canola or corn oil
- ½ onion (medium, chopped)

- 2 garlic cloves (minced)
- 1 tablespoon Worcestershire sauce
- 1 tablespoon brisket seasoning

Directions:

1. Whisk your ingredients all together in a saucepan.
2. Set up the grill for direct cooking
3. Let the grill heat at 350 degrees Fahrenheit for 15 minutes, with the lid closed.
4. Let your ingredients simmer on the grates till they come to a boil, then lower the heat.

5. Let it get nice and thick, and then take it off the grill, and let it cool

Nutrition:

- Calories: 40
- Protein: 10g
- Carbs: 4g

Carolina Mopping Sauce

Preparation Time: 5 minutes

Cooking Time: 5 minutes

Servings: 8 to 12

Ingredients:

- 1 cup cider vinegar
- 1 tablespoon hot sauce
- 1 tablespoon red pepper flakes
- 1 cup distilled white
- 1 teaspoon onion powder
- 1 teaspoon garlic powder
- 2 tablespoons brown sugar (packed)
- 1 teaspoon dry mustard
- ½ teaspoon salt
- ¼ teaspoon black pepper (ground)

Directions:

1. Simply mix all your ingredients together, and then store in an airtight fridge for a month.
2. If you need more heat, just add some more red pepper flakes.

Nutrition:

- Calories: 26
- Protein: 17g
- Carbs: 6g

Pulled Pork Mop Recipe

Preparation Time: 5 minutes

Cooking Time: 5 minutes

Servings: 8 to 12 **Ingredients:**

- 16 ounces cider vinegar
- 16 ounces vegetable oil
- 32 ounces water
- 1 cup ultra-dry rub
- 2 tablespoons Worcestershire sauce
- 2 tablespoons soy sauce

Directions:

1. Simply whisk all the ingredients together after dissolving your dry rub with some hot water.

Nutrition:

- Calories: 40
- Protein: 19g
- Carbs: 8g

Apple Butter and Fireball BBQ Sauce

Preparation Time: 10 minutes

Cooking Time: 60 minutes

Servings: 3

Ingredients:

- 1 tablespoon olive oil
- ½ yellow onion, diced
- 3 garlic cloves, minced
- 1 ½ cups apple butter
- ½ cup cinnamon whiskey, such as Fireball
- ½ cup ketchup
- 1/3 cup apple cider vinegar
- ½ cup brown sugar, packed
- 2 tablespoons Worcestershire sauce
- 1 teaspoon cayenne pepper flakes
- 1 teaspoon ground mustard
- 1 teaspoon ground black pepper
- 1 teaspoon salt

Directions:

1. Coat the bottom of a saucepan with the oil.
2. Add the garlic and onion and place on the stove over medium heat, sautéing the onions until they become translucent.
3. Pour the cinnamon whiskey into the saucepan with the tender vegetables and stir until well combined.
4. Bring the mixture to a boil before reducing the heat and simmering for 10 minutes, while stirring frequently.

5. While the mixture is simmering, combine the ketchup, apple butter, Worcestershire sauce, vinegar, mustard, brown sugar, salt, black pepper, and cayenne pepper in a mixing bowl.
6. Combine the mixture from Step 3 into the mixture from Step 2.
7. Turn the heat up and bring the mixture back to a boil, while stirring regularly. Once it boils, reduce the heat again and let it simmer for 25 to 30 minutes.
8. Take the saucepan off the heat and let it cool down. Use immediately or pour into mason jars and store in the fridge until ready to use.

Nutrition:

- Calories: 50
- Protein: 26g
- Carbs: 8g

Spicy and Sweet Jalapeno BBQ Sauce

Preparation Time: 10 minutes
Cooking Time: 30 minutes
Servings: 2
Ingredients:

- ½ cup butter, unsalted
- ½ cup brown sugar, packed
- 1 whole jalapeno, grilled for about 2 minutes
- 15 ounces tomato sauce, canned
- ½ cup apple cider vinegar
- 1 tablespoon Worcestershire sauce
- 1 tablespoon onion powder
- 1 tablespoon garlic powder
- 1 teaspoon salt
- 1 teaspoon ground mustard
- 1 teaspoon cumin
- ½ teaspoon ground cayenne pepper

Directions:

1. Place the butter in a saucepan. Set the pan on the stove over medium heat and melt the butter.
2. Stir in the brown sugar, bring to a boil, and boil for about 5 minutes.
3. Place the grilled jalapeno pepper into a blender. Add the tomato sauce and blend until there are no chunks left.
4. Transfer the tomato mixture into the butter mixture.
5. Add the Worcestershire sauce, onion powder, vinegar, ground mustard, salt, cayenne pepper, cumin, and garlic powder. Stir until well combined.

6. Let the mixture simmer for 30 minutes, making sure to stir the mixture frequently.
7. Remove the sauce from the heat and let it cool down a bit.
8. Use the sauce immediately or transfer to a mason jar. Store unused BBQ sauce in the fridge for up to 7 to 10 days.

Nutrition:

- Calories: 55
- Protein: 20g
- Carbs: 6g

Honey BBQ Sauce Preparation

Time: 10 minutes **Cooking**

Time: 35 minutes **Servings:** 3

Ingredients:

- 1 tablespoon dark brown sugar, packed
- 2 tablespoons chili powder
- 1 tablespoon smoked paprika
- 1 tablespoon sage, dried
- 1 tablespoon yellow mustard, ground
- 1 teaspoon kosher salt
- ½ teaspoon cayenne powder
- 1 small to medium-sized yellow onion, chopped roughly
- 8 ounces smoked bacon, chopped roughly
- 1 large shot glass bourbon
- 4 garlic cloves, chopped roughly
- ½ cup espresso, strongly brewed
- ½ cup coffee, strongly brewed
- 1 cup ketchup
- 2 tablespoon honey
- 1 tablespoon soy sauce

Directions:

1. Cook the bacon in a skillet over medium heat for about 8 to 10 minutes. Stir in the garlic and onion, and continue to cook for an additional 8 to 10 minutes.
2. Stir the brown sugar, chili powder, paprika, sage, salt, and cayenne powder into the bacon mixture until well mixed.

3. Add the bourbon to deglaze the pan. Remove the skillet from the heat and transfer to a blender or food processor.

4. Pour the espresso, coffee, honey, soy sauce, and ketchup into the food processor with the bacon mixture. Blend the mixture until it is completely smooth.

5. Transfer the BBQ sauce into a mason jar and close securely. Keep the sauce inside the fridge until it's ready to be used.

Nutrition:

- Calories: 45
- Protein: 20g
- Carbs: 4g

Hawaiian-Inspired BBQ Sauce

Preparation Time: 10 minutes **Cooking Time:** 30 minutes

Servings: 3

Ingredients:

- 1 ½ tablespoons ginger, grated finely
- 3 garlic cloves, minced
- 1 cup ketchup, all-natural
- ¼ cup dark brown sugar, packed
- ½ tablespoon dry mustard
- ½ cup soy sauce, low-sodium
- ½ teaspoon chili powder
- ¼ teaspoon white pepper
- ¼ cup orange juice, freshly squeezed
- 8 ounces crushed pineapple

Directions:

1. Place all the ingredients in a saucepan. Put the saucepan over the stove and let the ingredients boil.
2. Once boiling, reduce heat to a simmer.
3. Let the mixture simmer for about 35 to 40 minutes. The sauce should reduce by half. Once this occurs, take the saucepan off the heat.
4. Move the sauce to a mason jar if you do not intend to use it immediately. Store unused sauce in the fridge for up to 7 days.

Nutrition:

- Calories: 45 Protein: 20g Carbs: 7g

Root Beer BBQ Sauce

Preparation Time: 15 minutes

Cooking Time: 2 hours

Servings: 3

Ingredients:

- 2 tablespoons oil, vegetable or canola
- 1 small onion, diced
- 1 ½ cups root beer
- ¼ cup brown sugar, packed
- ¼ cup apple cider vinegar - ½ teaspoon cumin
- 15 ounces diced tomatoes, canned
- ½ to 1 teaspoon cayenne pepper

Directions:

1. Place the oil in a saucepan. Put the saucepan over the stove and let it heat.
2. Once warm, add the onions and sauté until they become translucent. Stir in the rest of the ingredients and bring the mixture to a boil while stirring frequently.
3. Once the mixture starts to boil, reduce the heat and let it simmer for about 40 minutes.
4. Take the saucepan off the heat and let it cool a little before blending the sauce in a blender until smooth.
5. Pour the sauce back into the saucepan and simmer for an hour. Remove the sauce from heat and let it cool completely.
6. Transfer the sauce into a pint-sized Mason jar and store in the fridge.

Nutrition:

- Calories: 28 Protein: 14g Carbs: 6g

Nectarine and Nutella Sundae

Preparation Time: 10 minutes **Cooking Time:** 25 minutes **Servings:** 4

Ingredients:

- 2 nectarines, halved and pitted
- 2 Teaspoon honey
- 4 Tablespoon Nutella
- 4 scoops vanilla ice cream
- 1/4 cup pecans, chopped
- Whipped cream, to top
- 4 cherries, to top

Directions:

1. Preheat pellet grill to 400°F.
2. Slice nectarines in half and remove the pits.
3. Brush the inside (cut side) of each nectarine half with honey.
4. Place nectarines directly on the grill grate, cut side down. Cook for 5-6 minutes, or until grill marks develop.
5. Flip nectarines and cook on the other side for about 2 minutes.
6. Remove nectarines from the grill and allow it to cool.
7. Fill the pit cavity on each nectarine half with 1 Tablespoon Nutella.
8. Place 1 scoop of ice cream on top of Nutella. Top with whipped cream, cherries, and sprinkle chopped pecans. Serve and enjoy!

Nutrition:

- Calories: 90 Fat: 3 g Cholesterol: 0 Carbohydrate: 15g Fiber: 0
- Sugar: 13 g Protein: 2 g

Cinnamon Sugar Donut Holes

Preparation Time: 10 minutes **Cooking Time:** 35 minutes

Servings: 4

Ingredients:

- 1/2 cup flour
- 1 Tablespoon cornstarch
- 1/2 Teaspoon baking powder
- 1/8 Teaspoon baking soda
- 1/8 Teaspoon ground cinnamon
- 1/2 Teaspoon kosher salt
- 1/4 cup buttermilk
- 1/4 cup sugar
- 1 1/2 Tablespoon butter, melted
- 1 egg
- 1/2 Teaspoon vanilla

Topping

- 2 Tablespoon sugar
- 1 Tablespoon sugar
- 1 Teaspoon ground cinnamon

Directions:

1. Preheat pellet grill to 350°F.
2. In a medium bowl, combine flour, cornstarch, baking powder, baking soda, ground cinnamon, and kosher salt. Whisk to combine.
3. In a separate bowl, combine buttermilk, sugar, melted butter, egg, and vanilla. Whisk until the egg is thoroughly combined.

4. Pour wet mixture into the flour mixture and stir. Stir just until combined, careful not to overwork the mixture.
5. Spray muffin tin with cooking spray.
6. Spoon 1 Tablespoon of donut mixture into each muffin hole.
7. Place the tin on the pellet grill grate and bake for about 18 minutes, or until a toothpick can come out clean.
8. Remove muffin tin from the grill and let rest for about 5 minutes.
9. In a small bowl, combine 1 Tablespoon sugar and 1 Teaspoon ground cinnamon.
10. Melt 2 Tablespoon of butter in a glass dish. Dip each donut hole in the melted butter, then mix and toss with cinnamon sugar. Place completed donut holes on a plate to serve.

Nutrition:

- Calories: 190
- Fat: 17 g
- Carbohydrate: 21 g
- Fiber: 1 g
- Sugar: 8 g
- Protein: 3 g

Pellet Grill Chocolate Chip Cookies

Preparation Time: 20 minutes

Cooking Time: 45 minutes **Servings:** 12

Ingredients:

- 1 cup salted butter, softened
- 1 cup of sugar
- 1 cup light brown sugar
- 2 Teaspoon vanilla extract
- 2 large eggs
- 3 cups all-purpose flour
- 1 Teaspoon baking soda
- 1/2 Teaspoon baking powder
- 1 Teaspoon natural sea salt
- 2 cups semi-sweet chocolate chips, or chunks

Directions:

1. Preheat pellet grill to 375°F.
2. Line a large baking sheet with parchment paper and set aside.
3. In a medium bowl, mix flour, baking soda, salt, and baking powder. Once combined, set aside.
4. In a stand mixer bowl, combine butter, white sugar, and brown sugar until combined. Beat in eggs and vanilla. Beat until fluffy.
5. Mix in dry ingredients, continue to stir until combined.
6. Add chocolate chips and mix thoroughly.
7. Roll 3 Tablespoon of dough at a time into balls and place them on your cookie sheet. Evenly space them apart, with about 2-3 inches in between each ball.

8. Place cookie sheet directly on the grill grate and bake for 20-25 minutes until the outside of the cookies is slightly browned.

9. Remove from grill and allow to rest for 10 minutes. Serve and enjoy!

Nutrition:

- Calories: 120
- Fat: 4
- Cholesterol: 7.8 mg
- Carbohydrate: 22.8 g
- Fiber: 0.3 g
- Sugar: 14.4 g
- Protein: 1.4 g

Delicious Donuts on a Grill

Preparation Time: 5 minutes

Cooking Time: 10 Minutes

Servings: 6

Ingredients:

- 1-1/2 cups sugar, powdered
- 1/3 cup whole milk
- 1/2 teaspoon vanilla extract
- 16 ounces of biscuit dough, prepared
- Oil spray for greasing
- 1cup chocolate sprinkles for sprinkling

Directions:

31. Take a medium bowl and mix sugar, milk, and vanilla extract.
32. Combine well to create a glaze.
33. Set the glaze aside for further use.
34. Place the dough onto the flat, clean surface.
35. Flat the dough with a rolling pin.
36. Use a ring mold, about an inch, and cut the hole in the center of each round dough.
37. Place the dough on a plate and refrigerate for 10 minutes.
38. Open the grill and install the grill grate inside it.
39. Close the hood.
40. Now, select the grill from the menu, and set the temperature to medium.
41. Set the time to 6 minutes.
42. Select start and begin preheating.
43. Remove the dough from the refrigerator and coat it with cooking spray from both sides.

44. When the unit beeps, the grill is preheated; place the adjustable amount of dough on the grill grate.

45. Close the hood, and cook for 3 minutes.

46. After 3 minutes, remove donuts and place the remaining dough inside.

47. Cook for 3 minutes.

48. Once all the donuts are ready, sprinkle chocolate sprinkles on top.

Nutrition:

- Calories: 400
- Total Fat: 11g
- Cholesterol: 1mg
- Sodium: 787mg
- Total Carbohydrate: 71.3g
- Total Sugars: 45.3g
- Protein: 5.7

Conclusion

Pellet grills are revolutionary and may forever change the way we cook.

These days, anyone can own a pellet grill since manufacturers meet the demand of clients from various backgrounds.

Modern pellet grills make cooking enjoyable and hassle-free.

It also eliminates guesswork thanks to the easy-to-follow recipes and the ability to remotely monitor and adjust your temperatures.

Whether you're an amateur home cook hosting a backyard cookout or a pitmaster at a barbecue competition, a wood pellet grill can easily become one of the most important appliances you can own to help you make flavorful meals with much less effort.

Although wood pellets grill isn't everyone's favorite choice, it's clear that a wood pellet grill is a must-have outdoor kitchen appliance. Whether you love smoking, grilling, roasting, barbecuing, or direct cooking of food, wood pellet grill is clearly versatile and has got you covered.

Cooking with a wood pellet grill allows you to choose the desired flavor of wood pellets to create the perfect smoke to flavor your food. Each wood pellet type has its personality and taste. The best part is you can use a single flavor or experiment with mixing and matching the flavors to invent your own combination.

Just like any cooking appliance, wood pellets have some drawbacks, but the benefits overshadow them. Therefore, it's definitely worth a try.

These days, one popular method of cooking is smoking, which many enthusiasts use. Proteins such as different kinds of meat, poultry, and fish would be ruined quickly if modern techniques in cooking are used. Smoking, on the other hand, is a process that takes a long time and low temperature, which thoroughly cooks the meat. The smoke, especially white smoke, greatly enhances the flavor of almost any food item. But more than that, smoking seals and preserves the nutrients in the food. Smoking is flexible and is one of the oldest techniques of making food.

Someone once dubbed smoking as a form of art. Only with the minimal period of consistent effort, any enthusiast can easily master the basics and advanced techniques. It is even said that once you master and improve on your expertise in smoking, you will not consider the other techniques in cooking to master anymore. But because of the many smoking techniques, you have to find a technique that is suitable for your temperament and style. You can do that by experimentation and trials of different smoking methods and different kinds of woods. Try cooking meat products for several hours using a heat source not directly on the meat. But you have to make sure that the smoke has a space to soak your meat and give it an access way out.

The picture of a good time with loved ones, neighbors, and friends having a backyard barbeque is a pretty sight, isn't it? Having a smoker- grill and some grilled and smoked recipes are excellent when you have visitors at home, because you can deliver both tasty food and magical moment on a summer night, for example. Hundreds of awesome recipes are available that you can try with a wood pellet smoker-grill! Experiment, improve, or make your own recipes – it is up to you. You can do it fast and easy. But if you want to be safe with the proven and tested ones, by all means do so. These recipes have been known to be just right to the taste, and they work every time. A combination of creating a correct impression the first time and every time and enjoying scrumptious food along the way will be your edge.

Another great thing about these recipes is that they are easy to prepare and do not require you to be a wizard in the kitchen. Simply by following a few easy steps and having the right ingredients at your disposal, you can use these recipes to make some delicious food in no time. So, try these recipes and spread the word! I'm sure this wood pellet smoker- grill recipe book will prove to be an invaluable gift to your loved ones, too!

Finally, while you will have fantastic smoking and grilling time with whichever wood pellet grill model you choose, the models are quite different. They hence offer different services and are suitable for different users. With new wood pellet grill series being produced each year, you need to shop smartly so that you buy a grill that perfectly fits you and meets all your needs.

If you are considering buying a grill yourself, then first you need to know the best kind of grills out in the market and what will suit you. You need to know how they work, compare, and which ones are trending. Traeger wood pellet grill is top on the markets and has many advantages over the standard cooking grill everyone has. New technology is coming out with better and better products to choose from, and if you don't upgrade your purchase and keep buying the same old stuff, then you will be left behind.

The Traeger grill provides a person which a great barbecuing experience with everyone, making food tastes better and cooking easier.

Now you no longer have to scour the web, hunting for your favorite wood pellet smoker-grill recipes. This book is a one-stop solution designed to eliminate all your struggles in finding the perfect wood pellet smoker-grill recipes for yourself and your loved ones.

NINJA FOODI GRILL

COOKBOOK

The Ultimate Step by Step Guide to Surprise Family and Friends by Cooking Delicious, Quick And Tasty Recipes for Indoor Grilling E Air Frying

GRILL ACADEMY

© Copyright 2020 - All rights reserved.

The content contained within this book may not be reproduced, duplicated or transmitted without direct written permission from the author or the publisher. Under no circumstances will any blame or legal responsibility be held against the publisher, or author, for any damages, reparation, or monetary loss due to the information contained within this book. Either directly or indirectly.

Legal Notice:

This book is copyright protected. This book is only for personal use. You cannot amend, distribute, sell, use, quote or paraphrase any part, or the content within this book, without the consent of the author or publisher.

Disclaimer Notice:

Please note the information contained within this document is for educational and entertainment purposes only. All effort has been executed to present accurate, up to date, and reliable, complete information. No warranties of any kind are declared or implied. Readers acknowledge that the author is not engaging in the rendering of legal, financial, medical or professional advice. The content within this book has been derived from various sources. Please consult a licensed professional before attempting any techniques outlined in this book.

By reading this document, the reader agrees that under no circumstances is the author responsible for any losses, direct or indirect, which are incurred as a result of the use of information contained within this document, including, but not limited to, errors, omissions, or inaccuracies.

Introduction

As a great cooking appliance with an excellent cooking facility, this Ninja Foodi grill is a 5 in 1 indoor grill with roast, bake, air fry, and dehydrator features with impressive performance. The inner pot of the Ninja Foodi has a non-stick surface that is safe to use even after years of utilization. The Ninja Foodi comes with a crisper basket, a grill grate, and a cooking pot. The smart probe is available with the pro package. The additional accessories can also be purchased like a roasting rack, griddle, vegetable tray, and dehydrating racks. The five modes allow different heat levels.

The production speciation is listed below:

- Dimensions: 17 inches L x 14 inches W x 11inhes H.
- Wattage: 1760.
- Capacity: 10 inches x 10 inches grills grate, 4-qt crisper basket, and 6-qt cooking pot.
- Cord Length: 3 feet.

The Grill Grate

The modes of grill grate are 5 and have 4 heat levels. The other functions mode allows setting time and temperature like air crisp, bake, roasting, and dehydrating.

The grill grate function is very easy, as it allows you to put food on to the grill grate, lock the hood, and choose mode from the low, medium, high, and max, and then set the time. For the other modes, the temperature is adjusted with time. Once the unit has started, the grill started to preheat for a specific time. After preheating is completed, the display shows "add food". You add food to the grill and close the top. The grill continues automatically.

The grill grate is added to the cooking pot inside the unit. The area for dripping is provided to collect dripping. The vent holes on the grill grate are used for airflow and drainage. The amazing grill-marked no odor or smoke during cooking. The grill surface is non-stick as well. You can grill chicken, steak, burger patties, vegetables, or any other food items like corn, broccoli, asparagus, etc.

Crisper Basket

The basket is usually 4-quarter, and it helps cook food items slightly perfect than the oven. You can put vegetables, chicken, meat, or any other thing in the basket. The basket's surface is non-stick, and it works very well without any issue of food sticking to the bottom. The basket also came in 6-quarter, which is coated with a ceramic non-stick coating. One of the great features of the basket is that when you open the lid, the grill time automatically pauses, and when you close the lid of the basket, the time automatically resumes. It is very easy to clean because of its non-stick ceramic coating, and it also came with a brush that is very helpful while cleaning and washing it. It is used mostly for air frying different food items.

The air fryer of the Ninja Foodi grill serves as a tiny convection oven with Ninja Foodi grill cyclonic drill technology, which cooks food in a faster and even way. It is the texture, taste, and smell of the food, which makes the Ninja Foodi grills a multi-kitchen appliance. The temperature of the Ninja Foodi grill ranges from 105 to 510 degrees F.

We can say that the food basket is easy to use, easy to clean; it automatically stops when checking to return the items. Our final suggestion is to introduce of a large version so that the food can easily be stored in the basket to serve large portions.

Pros of Using Ninja Foodi Grill

- It provides a hand free cooking experience.
- The grilling is done smoke, then a traditional backyard grill.
- The nutrients are lock in the food while air frying, grilling, roasting, or baking.
- It helps you achieve your diet goals, as it helps you prepare food with a very minimum amount of oil.
- It's an energy-saving appliance.
- The house environment remains odor-free.
- Even the cheapest cut of meats ate cooked to its tender perfection.
- It saves time.
- It saves money to buy spate appliance to air fry, dehydrate, grill or roast as it is a multi-tasker.

- It offers a stress-free cooking experience.
- The button functions are easy to use.
- Family meals can easily be prepared.
- It proved versatile and convenient.

Ninja Foodi Grill Unboxing

When you first open or unbox the Ninja Foodi grill it comes with a recipe guide, owner guide, product information, power cords, grill plate, grill brush, skewers, spatula, etc. main unit.

The grill unit holds a cooking pan, fry basket, splash guard, and grates.

You can set up the appliance by starting the cooking process in no time. The other accessories needed to buy separately.

Chapter 2

What Is Ninja Foodi Grill?

The Ninja Foodi is the most versatile and easy to use kitchen appliance you will ever own. It's an electric pressure cooker, sauté pan, air fryer, slow cooker, a rice cooker all in one. The combination of air fryer and pressure cooker will cook your food faster and more efficiently than any other tool in your kitchen. You can make all your favorite meals in the Ninja Foodi Cooker.

The Ninja Foodi Cooker is top-notch. You will be fascinated by how well it cooks your favorite food. It works fast; it is easy to set up and use in the kitchen. Therefore, if you're new to using a multi-cooker, you'll get used to it quickly and easily. You can use your multi-cooker manually or opt for some of the seven preset programs. Programs. An easy-to-use interface allows you to select your desired cooking program easily.

Ninja Foodi Functionalities

The list below offers a brief look at all the core buttons´funcionalities that should help you understand what each of the main buttons does.

Pressure

Let's first talk about the single feature that you will be using most of the time. The Pressure function will allow you to use your Ninja Foodi as a Pressure Cooker appliance and cook your meals as you would in an electric pressure cooker such as the Ninja Foodi.

In this feature, foods are cooked at high temperatures under pressure.

Just make sure to be careful when releasing the pressure! Otherwise, you might harm yourself.

Steam

Asides from Air Crisp, the Steam Function is probably one of the healthiest cooking options available in the Foodi!

The basic principle is as follows: water is boiled inside the Ninja Foodi that generates a good steam amount. This hot steam is then used to cook your ingredients kept in a steaming rack situated at the top of your pot's inner chamber.

Steaming is perfect for vegetables and other tender foods as it allows you to preserve the nutrients while maintaining a nice crispy correctly.

Asides from vegetables, however, the Steam function can also be used for cooking various fish and seafood, which are much more delicate than other red meats and chicken.

The steaming fish process is the same; all you have to do is place them on the steaming rack.

Steaming the fish helps to preserve the flavor and moisture as well perfectly.

Slow Cooker

Despite popular belief, some foods tend to taste a whole lot better when slowly cooked over a shallow temperature for hours on end. This is why Slow Cookers, such as the Crockpot, are so popular amongst chefs and house makers!

The Slow Cooker feature of the Ninja Foodi allows you to achieve the same result a different appliance.

Ideal scenarios to use the Slow Cooker function would be when you want to cook your foods for longer to bring out the intense flavor of spices and herbs in stews, soups, and casseroles.

Since it takes a lot of time to Slow Cook, you should prepare and toss the ingredients early on before your feeding time.

For example, if you want to have your Slow Cooker meal for breakfast, prepare ingredients the night before and add them to your Foodi. The Foodi will do its magic and have the meal prepared by morning.

The Slow Cooker feature also comes with a HIGH or LOW setting that allows you to decide how long you want your meal to simmer.

Air Crisp

This is probably the feature that makes the Ninja Foodi so revolutionary and awesome to use! The Tender crisp lid that comes as a part of the Ninja Foodi allows you to use the appliance as the perfect Air Fryer device.

Using the Tender crisp lid and Air Crisp mode, the appliance will let you bake, roast, broil meals to perfection using just the power of superheated air! In the end, you will get perfectly caramelized, heartwarming dishes.

The Foodi comes with a dedicated crisping basket specifically designed for this purpose, which optimizes the way meals are air fried in the Foodi.

But the best part of all of these is probably the fact that it is using the Air Crisp feature; you will be able to cook your meals using almost none to minimal amount of oil!

It is also possible to combine both the pressure-cooking mechanism and Air Crisp function to create unique and flavorful dishes.

The Pressure-cooking phase will help you to seal the delicious juices of the meal inside the meat. Simultaneously, the crisping lid and Air Crisp mechanism will allow you to cook/roast your meal to perfection, giving a nice heartfelt crispy finish.

This combined method is also amazing when roasting whole chicken meat or roasts, as all the moisture remains intact, and the final result turns out to be a dramatic crispy finish.

Sear/Sauté

The Browning/Sauté or Sear/Sauté mode of the Ninja Foodi provides you with the means to brown your meat before cooking it using just a little oil. This is similar to when you are browning meat on a stovetop frying pan. And keeping that in mind, the Ninja Foodie's browning model comes with five different Stove Top temperature settings that allow you to set your desired settings with ease.

Asides from browning meat, the different Stove Top temperatures also allow you to gently simmer your foods, cook or even sear them at very high temperatures.

Searing is yet another way to infuse your meat's delicious flavors inside and give an extremely satisfying result.

This particular model is also excellent if you are in the mode for a quick Sautéed vegetable snack to go along with your main course.

Bake/Roast

To those who love to bake, this function is a dream come true! The Bake/Roast function allows the Foodi to be used as a traditional convection oven. This means you will be do anything that you might do with a general everyday oven! If you are in the mode to bake amazing cakes or casseroles, the Foodi has got you covered!

Broil

The broil function's primary purpose is to allow you to use your appliance like an oven broiler and slightly brown the top of your dish if required. If you are in the mood for roasting a fine piece of pork loin to perfection or broiling your dish until the cheese melts and oozes, this mode is the perfect one to go with!

Dehydrate

In some more premium models of the Ninja Foodi appliance, you will notice a function labeled as "Dehydrate." This particular function is best suited for simple dried snacks such as dried apple slices, banana chips, jerky, etc. As you can probably guess, this function's core idea is to suck out the moisture and dehydrate your ingredient into a hearty edible snack.

Start/Stop Button

This particular button's function is pretty straightforward; it allows you to initiate or stop the cooking process.

How to Use the Ninja Foodi Grill

When you are cooking for the first time with your Ninja Foodi Grill, you must first wash the detachable cooking parts with warm soapy water to remove any oil and debris. Let them air dry and place them back inside once you are ready to cook. An easy-to-follow instruction guide comes with each unit, so make sure to go over it before cooking.

Position your grill on a level and secure surface. Please leave at least 6 inches of space around it, especially at the back where the air intake vent and air socket are located. Ensure that the splatter guard is installed whenever the grill is in use. This is a wire mesh that covers the heating element on the inside of the lid.

Grilling

Plug your unit into an outlet and power on the grill.

Use the grill grate over the cooking pot and choose the grill function. This has four default temperature settings of low at 400°F, medium at 450°F, high at 500°F, and max at 510°F.

Set the time needed to cook. You may check the grilling cheat sheet that comes with your unit to guide you with the time and temperature settings. It is best to check the food regularly depending on the doneness you prefer and to avoid overcooking.

Once the required settings are selected, press start and wait for the digital display to show 'add food.' The unit will start to preheat, similar to an oven, and will show the progress through the display. This step takes about 8 minutes.

If you need to check the food or flip it, the timer will pause and resume once the lid is closed.

The screen will show 'Done' once the timer and cooking have been completed. Power off the unit and unplug the device. Leave the hood open to let the unit cool faster.

Roasting

Remove the grill grates and use the cooking pot that comes with the unit. You may also purchase their roasting rack for this purpose.

Press the roast option and set the timer between 1 to 4 hours depending on the recipe requirements.

The food will preheat for 3 minutes regardless of the time you have set.

Once ready, place the meat directly on the roasting pot or rack.

Check occasionally for doneness. A meat thermometer is another useful tool to get your meats perfectly cooked.

Baking

Remove the grates and use the cooking pot. Choose the bake setting and set your preferred temperature and time. Preheating will take about 3 minutes. Once done with preheating, you may put the ingredients directly on the cooking pot, or use your regular baking tray. An 8-inch baking tray can fit inside as well as similar-sized oven-safe containers.

Air Frying / Air Crisping

Put the crisper basket in and close the lid.

Press the air crisp or air fry option, then the start button. The default temperature is set at 390° F and will preheat at about 3 minutes. You can adjust the temperature and time by pressing the buttons beside these options.If you do not need to preheat, press the air crisp button a second time, and the display will show you the 'add food' message.

Put the food inside and shake or turn every 10 minutes. Use oven mitts or tongs with silicone tips when doing this.

Dehydrating

Place the first layer of food directly on the cooking pot.

Add the crisper basket and add one more layer.

Choose the dehydrate setting and set the timer between 7 to 10 hours.

You can check the progress from time to time.

Cooking Frozen Foods

Choose the MEDIUM heat, which is 450° F using the grill option. You may also use the air crisp option if you are cooking fries, vegetables, and other frozen foods. Set the time needed for your recipe. Add a few minutes to compensate for the thawing.

Flip or shake after a few minutes to cook the food evenly.

Cleaning and Maintenance

Components are dishwasher-safe and are fabricated with a non-stick ceramic coating to make clean-up and maintenance easier. Plus, the grill conveniently comes with a plastic cleaning brush with a scraper at the other end.

Cleaning Tips

Let the grill cool down completely and ensure that it is unplugged from the power outlet before cleaning the unit.

Take out the splatter guard, grill grates, and cooking pot, and soak in soapy water for a few hours to let the debris soften and make cleaning easier. Wash only the removable parts.

Gently brush off dirt and debris using the plastic brush that comes with your grill. Use the other end of the brush to dislodge food in hard to reach areas.

Let the parts dry thoroughly.

Clean the insides and exterior of the unit with a clean damp cloth.

Maintenance Tips

Always keep your unit clean, especially before putting in a new batch for cooking. You should clean the parts and the unit after each use.

Never use cleaning instruments or chemicals that are too harsh and can damage the coating.

Keep the electrical cords away from children and any traffic in your kitchen.

Avoid getting the unit and electrical components wet and place it away from areas that constantly get soaked or damp.

Always unplug the unit if not in use.

Troubleshooting

Smoke coming out of the grill

Although the Ninja Foodi is virtually smokeless as advertised, you may see some smoke from time to time for many reasons.

One is the type of oil you use for cooking. Ideally, canola, grape seed, and avocado oil should be used since they have a high smoke point. This means that they do not produce smoke or burn at high temperatures. Other oils with high smoke points include corn, almond, safflower, sesame, and sunflower oils.

Another reason is the accumulation of grease at the bottom of the pot. If you continuously cook foods that produce a lot of grease and oil, this will burn and create smoke—empty and clean the pot before cooking the next batch.

The grill is showing 'Add Food.'

This means that the unit has finished preheating and that you can now put food inside the grill.

The control panel is showing 'Shut Lid.'

Try opening the lid and closing it securely until the message is gone.

Unit is unresponsive and only showing 'E' on the panel.

Your unit is damaged, and you need to contact customer service.

Chapter 3

Breakfast

1. Grilled French Toast

Preparation Time: 10 minutes
Cooking Time: 8 minutes
Servings: 3
Ingredients
- 3- 1-inch slices challah bread
- 2 eggs
- Juice of ½ orange
- ½ quart strawberries, quartered
- 1-tablespoon honey
- 1-tablespoon balsamic vinegar

- 1-teaspoon orange zest
- 1/2 sprig fresh rosemary
- ½-teaspoon vanilla extract
- Salt to taste
- 1/4 cup heavy cream
- Fine sugar, for dusting, optional

Directions
1. Spread a foil sheet on a working surface.
2. Add strawberries, balsamic, orange juice, rosemary, and zest.
3. Fold the foil edges to make a pocket.
4. Whisk egg with cream, honey, vanilla, and a pinch of salt.
5. Dip and soak the bread slices in this mixture and shake off the excess.
6. Prepare and preheat the Ninja Foodi Grill in the medium-temperature setting.
7. Once it is preheated, open the lid and place the bread slices and the foil packet on the grill.
8. Cover the Ninja Foodi Grill's lid and let them grill on the "Grilling Mode" for 2 minutes in batches.
9. Flip the bread slices and continue grilling for another 2 minutes.
10. Serve the bread with the strawberry mix on top.
11. Enjoy.

Nutrition
- Calories: 387
- Total Fat: 6 g
- Saturated Fat: 9.9 g
- Cholesterol: 41 mg
- Sodium: 154 mg
- Total Carbs: 37.4 g
- Fiber: 2.9 g
- Sugar: 15.3 g
- Protein: 14.6 g

2. Sausage with Eggs

Preparation Time: 10 minutes
Cooking Time: 10 minutes
Servings: 4

Ingredients

- 4 sausage links
- 2 cups chopped kale
- 1 medium sweet yellow onion
- 4 eggs
- 1-cup mushrooms - Olive oil

Directions

1. Prepare and preheat the Ninja Foodi Grill in a High-temperature setting.
2. Once it is preheated, open the lid and place the sausages on the grill. Cover the Ninja Foodi Grill's lid and let it grill on the "Grilling Mode" for 2 minutes.
3. Flip the sausages and continue grilling for another 3 minutes
4. Now spread the onion, mushrooms, and kale in an iron skillet.
5. Crack the eggs in between the sausages.
6. Bake this mixture for 5 minutes the oven at 350 degrees F.
7. Serve warm and fresh.

Nutrition

- Calories: 212
- Total Fat: 11.8 g
- Saturated Fat: 2.2 g
- Cholesterol: 23mg
- Sodium: 321 mg
- Total Carbs: 14.6 g
- Dietary Fiber: 4.4 g
- Sugar: 8 g
- Protein: 17.3 g

3. Espresso Glazed Bagels

Preparation Time: 10 minutes
Cooking Time: 8 minutes
Servings: 4
Ingredients

- 4 bagels, split in half
- 1/4 cup coconut milk
- 1-cup fine sugar
- 2 tablespoons black coffee
- 2 tablespoons coconut flakes

Directions

1. Prepare and preheat the Ninja Foodi Grill on a medium-temperature setting.
2. Once it is preheated, open the lid and place 2 bagels in the grill.
3. Cover the Ninja Foodi Grill's lid and let it grill on the "Grilling Mode" for 2 minutes.
4. Flip the bagel and continue grilling for another 2 minutes.
5. Grill the remaining bagels in a similar way.
6. Whisk the rest of the ingredients in a bowl well.
7. Drizzle this sauce over the grilled bagels.
8. Serve.

Nutrition

- Calories: 412
- Total Fat: 24.8 g
- Saturated Fat: 12.4 g
- Cholesterol: 3 mg
- Sodium: 132 mg
- Total Carbs: 43.8 g
- Dietary Fiber: 3.9 g
- Sugar: 2.5 g
- Protein: 18.9 g

4. Bruschetta Portobello Mushrooms

Preparation Time: 10 minutes
Cooking Time: 8 minutes
Servings: 6
Ingredients

- 2 cups cherry tomatoes cut in half
- 3 tablespoons red onion, diced
- 3 tablespoons fresh basil shredded
- Salt and black pepper to taste
- 4 tablespoons butter
- 1 teaspoon dried oregano
- 6 large Portobello Mushrooms, caps only, washed and dried
- For Balsamic glaze:
- 2 teaspoons brown sugar
- 1/4 cup balsamic vinegar

Directions

1. Start by preparing the balsamic glaze and take all its ingredients in a saucepan.
2. Stir cook this mixture for 8 minutes on medium heat then remove from the heat.
3. Take the mushrooms and brush them with the prepared glaze.
4. Stuff the remaining ingredients into the mushrooms.
5. Prepare and preheat the Ninja Foodi Grill in the medium-temperature setting.
6. Once it is preheated, open the lid and place the stuffed mushrooms in grill with their cap side down.
7. Cover the Ninja Foodi Grill's lid and let it grill on the "Grilling Mode" for 8 minutes.
8. Serve.

Nutrition

- Calories: 331 Total Fat: 2.5 g Saturated Fat: 0.5 g
- Cholesterol: 35 mg Sodium: 595 mg Total Carbs: 69 g
- Fiber: 12.2 g Sugar: 12.5 g Protein: 8.7g

5. Sausage Mixed Grill

Preparation Time: 5 minutes
Cooking Time: 22 minutes
Servings: 4

Ingredients

- 8 mini bell peppers
- 2 heads radicchio, each cut into 6 wedges
- Canola oil, for brushing
- Sea salt
- Freshly ground black pepper
- 6 breakfast sausage links
- 6 hot or sweet Italian sausage links

Directions

1. Insert the grill grate and close the hood. Select grill, set the temperature to max, and set the time to 22 minutes. Select start
2. Stop to begin preheating.
3. While the unit is preheating, brush the bell peppers and radicchio with the oil. Season with salt and black pepper.
4. When the unit beeps to signify it has preheated, place the bell peppers and radicchio on the grill grate close the hood and cook for 10 minutes, without flipping.
5. Meanwhile, poke the sausages with a fork or knife and brush them with some of the oil.
6. After 10 minutes, remove the vegetables and set aside. Decrease the temperature to low. Place the sausages on the grill grate close the hood and cook for 6 minutes.
7. Flip the sausages. Close the hood and cook for 6 minutes more. Remove the sausages from the grill grate.
8. Serve the sausages and vegetables on a large cutting board or serving tray.

Nutrition

- Calories: 473 Fat: 34g Saturated Fat: 11g Cholesterol: 73mg
- Sodium: 1051mg Carbohydrates: 14g Fiber: 2g Protein: 28g

6. Sausage and Egg Loaded Breakfast Pockets

Preparation Time: 15 minutes
Cooking Time: 23 minutes
Servings: 4

Ingredients

- 1 (6-ounce) package ground breakfast sausage, crumbled
- 3 large eggs, lightly beaten
- ⅓ cup diced red bell pepper
- ⅓ cup thinly sliced scallions (green part only)
- Sea salt
- Freshly ground black pepper
- 1 (16-ounce) package pizza dough
- All-purpose flour, for dusting
- 1 cup shredded cheddar cheese
- 2 tablespoons canola oil

Directions

1. Select roast, set the temperature to 375°f, and set the time to 15 minutes. Select start
2. Stop to begin preheating.
3. When the unit beeps to signify it has preheated, place the sausage directly in the pot.
4. Close the hood, and cook for 10 minutes, checking the sausage every 2 to 3 minutes, breaking apart larger pieces with a wooden spoon.
5. After 10 minutes, pour the eggs, bell pepper, and scallions into the pot.
6. Stir to evenly incorporate with the sausage.
7. Close the hood and let the eggs cook for the remaining 5 minutes, stirring occasionally.
8. Transfer the sausage and egg mixture to a medium bowl to cool slightly. Season with salt and pepper.
9. Insert the crisper basket and close the hood.
10. Select air crisp, set the temperature to 350°f, and set the time to 8 minutes. Select start

11. Stop to begin preheating.
12. Meanwhile, divide the dough into four equal pieces.
13. Lightly dust a clean work surface with flour. Roll each piece of dough into a 5-inch round of even thickness.
14. Divide the sausage-egg mixture and cheese evenly among each round. Brush the outside edge of the dough with water.
15. Fold the dough over the filling, forming a half circle. Pinch the edges of the dough together to seal in the filling. Brush both sides of each pocket with the oil.
16. When the unit beeps to signify it has preheated, place the breakfast pockets in the basket. Close the hood and cook for 6 to 8 minutes, or until golden brown.

Nutrition
- Calories: 639
- Fat: 40g
- Saturated Fat: 8g
- Cholesterol: 169mg
- Sodium: 765mg
- Carbohydrates: 50g
- Fiber: 4g
- Protein: 24g

7. Grilled Cinnamon Toast with Berries and Whipped Cream

Preparation Time: 15 minutes
Cooking Time: 10 minutes
Servings: 4

Ingredients

- 1 (15-ounce) can full-
- Fat coconut milk, refrigerated overnight
- ½ tablespoon powdered sugar
- 1½ teaspoons vanilla extract, divided
- 1 cup halved strawberries
- 1 tablespoon maple syrup, plus more for garnish
- 1 tablespoon brown sugar, divided
- ¾ cup lite coconut milk
- 2 large eggs
- ½ teaspoon ground cinnamon
- 2 tablespoons unsalted butter, at room temperature
- 4 slices challah bread

Directions

1. Turn the chilled can of full-Fat coconut milk upside down (do not shake the can), open the bottom, and pour out the liquid coconut water.
2. Scoop the remaining solid coconut cream into a medium bowl. Using an electric hand mixer, whip the cream for 3 to 5 minutes, until soft peaks form.
3. Add the powdered sugar and ½ teaspoon of the vanilla to the coconut cream and whip it again until creamy. Place the bowl in the refrigerator.
4. Insert the grill grate and close the hood. Select grill, set the temperature to max, and set the time to 15 minutes. Select start
5. Stop to begin preheating.
6. While the unit is preheating, combine the strawberries with the maple syrup and toss to coat evenly. Sprinkle evenly with ½ tablespoon of the brown sugar.

7. In a large shallow bowl, whisk together the lite coconut milk, eggs, the remaining 1 teaspoon of vanilla, and cinnamon.
8. When the unit beeps to signify it has preheated, place the strawberries on the grill grate. Gently press the fruit down to maximize grill marks. Close the hood and grill for 4 minutes without flipping.
9. Meanwhile, butter each slice of bread on both sides. Place one slice in the egg mixture and let it soak for 1 minute. Flip the slice over and soak it for another minute.
10. Repeat with the remaining bread slices. Sprinkle each side of the toast with the remaining ½ tablespoon of brown sugar.
11. After 4 minutes, remove the strawberries from the grill and set aside. Decrease the temperature to high.
12. Place the bread on the grill grate close the hood and cook for 4 to 6 minutes, until golden and caramelized. Check often to ensure desired doneness.
13. Place the toast on a plate and top with the strawberries and whipped coconut cream. Drizzle with maple syrup, if desired.

Nutrition
- Calories: 386
- Fat: 19g
- Saturated Fat: 12g
- Cholesterol: 97mg
- Sodium: 143mg
- Carbohydrates: 49g
- Fiber: 2g
- Protein: 7g

8. Avocado Eggs

Preparation Time: 10 minutes
Cooking Time: 5 minutes
Servings: 2

Ingredients

- 1 ripe avocado
- 1 pinch of barbecue rub
- 2 eggs
- Salt and pepper, to taste
- 1 red jalapeño, finely diced
- 1 tomato, chopped

Directions

1. Slice avocado in half and remove its pit.
2. Remove some flesh from the center then crack an egg into the halves.
3. Drizzle barbecue rub, salt, pepper, jalapeno and tomato on top.
4. Prepare and preheat the Ninja Foodi Grill in a High-temperature setting.
5. Once it is preheated, open the lid and place the stuffed avocado in grill with their skin side down.
6. Cover the Ninja Foodi Grill's lid and let it grill on the "Grilling Mode" for 5 minutes.
7. Serve.

Nutrition

- Calories: 322
- Total Fat: 11.8 g
- Saturated Fat: 2.2 g
- Cholesterol: 56 mg
- Sodium: 321 mg
- Total Carbs: 14.6 g
- Dietary Fiber: 4.4 g
- Sugar: 8 g Protein: 17.3 g

9. Coconut French Toast

Preparation Time: 10 minutes
Cooking Time: 16 minutes
Servings: 5
Ingredients

- 1/4 cup milk
- 3 large eggs
- 1 (12-oz. loaf bread- 10 slices
- 1/4 cup sugar
- Cooking spray
- 1 cup of coconut milk
- 10 (1/4-inch-thick slices pineapple, peeled
- 1/2 cup coconut flakes

Directions

1. Whisk the coconut milk with sugar, eggs, and fat-free milk in a bowl.
2. Dip the bread in this mixture and keep it aside for 1 minute.
3. Prepare and preheat the Ninja Foodi Grill on medium-temperature setting.
4. Once it is preheated, open the lid and place 5 bread slices on the grill.
5. Cover the Ninja Foodi Grill's lid and let it grill on the "Grilling Mode" for 2 minutes.
6. Flip the slices and continue grilling for another 2 minutes.
7. Cook the remaining 5 slices in a similar way.
8. Now grill 5 pineapples slices on the grill for 2 minutes per side.
9. Grill the remaining pineapple in the same way.
10. Serve the bread with pineapple on top.
11. Garnish with coconut and serve.

Nutrition

- Calories: 197 Total Fat: 15.4 g Saturated Fat: 4.2 g
- Cholesterol: 168 mg Sodium: 203 mg Total Carbs: 58.5 g
- Sugar: 1.1 g Fiber: 4 g Protein: 7.9 g

10. Bacon-Herb Grit

Preparation Time: 10 minutes
Cooking Time: 10 minutes
Servings: 4
Ingredients

- 1 tablespoon minced fresh
- 2 teaspoons chopped fresh parsley
- 1/2 teaspoon garlic powder
- 1/2 teaspoon black pepper
- 3 bacon slices, cooked and crumbled
- 1/2 cup shredded cheddar cheese
- 4 cups instant grits
- Cooking spray

Directions

1. Start by mixing the first seven ingredients in a suitable bowl.
2. Spread this mixture in a 10-inch baking pan and refrigerate for 1 hour.
3. Flip the pan on a plate and cut the grits mixture into 4 triangles.
4. Prepare and preheat the Ninja Foodi Grill in the medium-temperature setting.
5. Once it is preheated, open the lid and place the grit slices in the grill.
6. Cover the Ninja Foodi Grill's lid and let it grill on the "Grilling Mode" for 5 minutes per side.
7. Serve.

Nutrition

- Calories: 138 Total Fat: 9.7 g
- Saturated Fat: 4.7 g Cholesterol: 181 mg
- Sodium: 245 mg Total Carbs: 32.5 g
- Fiber: 0.3 g Sugar: 1.8 g Protein: 10.3 g

Chapter 4

Snacks

1. Crispy Brussels Leaves
Preparation Time: 5-10 minutes
Cooking Time: 12 minutes
Servings: 4
Ingredients
- 1-pound Brussels sprouts, halved
- 2 tablespoons olive oil, extra-virgin
- ½ teaspoon ground black pepper

- 1 teaspoon sea salt - 6 slices bacon, chopped

Directions
1. In a mixing bowl, toss the Brussels sprouts, olive oil, salt, black pepper, and bacon. Take ninja foodi grill, arrange it over your kitchen platform, and open the top lid.
2. Arrange the crisping basket inside the pot.
3. Press "air crisp" and adjust the temperature to 390°f. Adjust the timer to 12 minutes and then press "start
4. Stop." Ninja foodi will start pre-heating. Ninja foodi is preheated and ready to cook when it starts to beep. After you hear a beep, open the top lid.
5. Arrange the Brussels sprout mixture directly inside the basket.
6. Close the top lid and cook for 6 minutes. After 6 minutes, shake the basket and close the top lid and cook for another 6 minutes.
7. Serve warm.

Nutrition
- Calories: 279 Fat: 1 5g Saturated Fat: 4g Trans Fat: 0g
- Carbohydrates: 15g Fiber: 4g Sodium: 874mg Protein: 15g

2. Cajuned Eggplant Appetizer

Preparation Time: 5-10 minutes
Cooking Time: 10 minutes
Servings: 4
Ingredients

- 2 tablespoons lime juice
- 3 teaspoons Cajun seasoning
- 2 small eggplants, cut into slices (1/2 inch)
- 1/4 cup olive oil

Directions:
1. Coat the eggplant slices with the oil, lemon juice, and Cajun seasoning.
2. Take ninja foodi grill, arrange it over your kitchen platform, and open the top lid.
3. Arrange the grill grate and close the top lid.
4. Press "grill" and select the "med" grill function. Adjust the timer to 10 minutes and then press "start
5. Stop." Ninja foodi will start pre-heating.
6. Ninja foodi is preheated and ready to cook when it starts to beep. After you hear a beep, open the top lid.
7. Arrange the eggplant slices over the grill grate.
8. Close the top lid and cook for 5 minutes. Now open the top lid, flip the eggplant slices.
9. Close the top lid and cook for 5 more minutes.
10. Divide into serving plates.
11. Serve warm.

Nutrition:

- Calories: 362 Fat: 11g
- Saturated Fat: 3g Trans Fat: 0g
- Carbohydrates: 16g Fiber: 1g
- Sodium: 694mg Protein: 8g

3. Grilled Honey Carrots

Preparation Time: 15 minutes
Cooking Time: 10 minutes
Servings: 4-5

Ingredients

- 2 tablespoons melted butter
- 6 carrots, peeled, cut lengthwise
- 1 tablespoon parsley, chopped
- 1 tablespoon rosemary, chopped
- 1 tablespoon honey
- 1 teaspoon kosher salt

Directions

1. Take ninja foodi grill, arrange it over your kitchen platform, and open the top lid.
2. Arrange the grill grate and close the top lid.
3. Press "grill" and select the "max" grill function. Adjust the timer to 10 minutes and then press "start
4. Stop." Ninja foodi will start preheating.
5. Ninja foodi is preheated and ready to cook when it starts to beep. After you hear a beep, open the top lid.
6. Arrange the carrots over the grill grate.
7. Close the top lid and cook for 5 minutes. Now open the top lid, flip the carrots.
8. Close the top lid and cook for 5 more minutes.
9. Serve warm.

Nutrition

- Calories: 82 Fat: 4g
- Saturated Fat: 1g Trans Fat: 0g
- Carbohydrates: 5g
- Fiber: 3g
- Sodium: 186mg
- Protein: 0.5g

4. Molten Lava Cakes

Preparation Time: 10 Minutes
Cooking Time: 13 Minutes
Servings: 4
Ingredients:

- 1 ½ tbsp. self-rising flour
- 3 ½ tbsp. baker's sugar
- 3 ½ oz. unsalted butter
- 3 ½ oz. dark chocolate, chopped
- 2 eggs

Directions:

1. Grease 4 ramekins with cooking spray and keep them aside.
2. First, melt the butter with dark chocolate in a glass bowl by heating in the microwave for 3 minutes.
3. Whisk eggs and sugar in a mixer until fluffy and pale.
4. Stir in melted chocolate, and flour then mix well until smooth.
5. Divide the chocolate batter in the ramekins and place these ramekins in the Ninja oven.
6. Seal the Ninja oven by closing its lid.
7. Rotate the Ninja Food i dial to select the "Air Fry" mode.
8. Press the Time button and again use the dial to set the cooking time to 10 minutes.
9. Now press the Temp button and rotate the dial to set the temperature at 375 degrees F.
10. Serve.

Nutrition:

- Calories: 317
- Total Fat: 11.9 g
- Carbs: 14.8 g
- Fiber: 1.1 g
- Sugar: 8.3 g
- Protein: 5 g

5. Fried Oreos

Preparation Time: 10 Minutes
Cooking Time: 4 Minutes
Servings: 4
Ingredients:

- 1 crescent sheet roll
- 9 Oreo cookies

Directions:

1. Spread the crescent sheet roll and cut it into 9 squares of equal size.
2. Place one Oreo cookie at the center of each square and wrap the crescent sheets around the cookies.
3. Place these wrapped cookies in the Air Fryer.
4. Transfer the cookies to the Ninja oven and Close its lid.
5. Rotate the Ninja Food i dial to select the "Air Fry" mode.
6. Press the Time button and again use the dial to set the cooking time to 4 minutes.
7. Now press the Temp button and rotate the dial to set the temperature at 360 degrees F.
8. Serve fresh.

Nutrition:

- Calories: 295
- Total Fat: 3 g
- Carbs: 10 g
- Fiber: 1 g
- Sugar: 5 g
- Protein: 1g

6. Chocolate Chip Cookie

Preparation Time: 10 Minutes
Cooking Time: 12 Minutes
Servings: 6
Ingredients

- 1/2 cup butter, softened
- 1/2 cup sugar
- 1/2 cup brown sugar
- 1 egg
- 1 tsp. vanilla
- 1/2 tsp. baking soda
- 1/4 tsp. salt
- 1 1/2 cups flour, preferably all-purpose
- 1 cup of chocolate chips

Directions

1. Grease the Ninja baking pan with cooking spray.
2. Beat butter with sugar and brown sugar in a mixing bowl.
3. Stir in vanilla, egg, salt, flour, and baking soda, then mix well.
4. Fold in chocolate chips then knead this dough a bit.
5. Spread the dough in the prepared baking pan evenly.
6. Transfer this pan to the Ninja oven and Close its lid.
7. Rotate the Ninja Foodi dial to select the "Bake" mode.
8. Press the Time button and again use the dial to set the cooking time to 12 minutes.
9. Now press the Temp button and rotate the dial to set the temperature at 400 degrees F.
10. Serve oven fresh.

Nutrition:

- Calories: 253 Fat: 8.9 g
- Carbs: 24.7 g Fiber: 1.2 g
- Sugar: 11.3 g Protein: 5.3 g

7. Blueberry Hand Pies

Preparation Time: 10 Minutes
Cooking Time: 25 Minutes
Servings: 6

Ingredients

- 1 cup blueberries
- 2.5 tbsp. caster sugar
- 1 tsp. lemon juice
- 1 pinch salt
- 14 oz. refrigerated pie crust
- water - vanilla sugar to sprinkle on top

Directions

1. Toss the blueberries with salt, lemon juice, and sugar in a medium bowl.
2. Spread the pie crust into a round sheet and cut 6-4 inch circles out of it. Add a tbsp. of blueberry filling at the center of each circle.
3. Moisten the edges of these circles and fold them in half then pinch their edges together.
4. Press the edges using a fork to crimp its edges.
5. Place the hand pieces in the Air Fryer and spray them with cooking oil.
6. Drizzle the vanilla sugar over the hand pies.
7. Transfer the hand pies on the Air Fryer to the Ninja oven and Close its lid.
8. Rotate the Ninja Food i dial to select the "Air Fry" mode.
9. Press the Time button and again use the dial to set the cooking time to 25 minutes.
10. Now press the Temp button and rotate the dial to set the temperature at 400 degrees F. Serve fresh.

Nutrition

- Calories: 327 Fat: 31.1 g Carbs: 49 g Sugar: 12.4 g
- Fiber: 1.8 g Protein: 13.5 g

8. Cherry Jam Tarts

Preparation Time: 10 Minutes
Cooking Time: 40 Minutes
Servings: 12
Ingredients

- 2 sheets shortcrust pastry

Frangipane

- 4 oz. butter softened
- 4 oz. golden caster sugar
- 1 egg
- 1 tbsp. plain flour
- 4 oz. ground almonds
- 3 oz. cherry jam

Icing

- 1 cup icing sugar
- 12 glacé cherries

Directions:

1. Grease the 12 cups of the muffin tray with butter.
2. Roll the puff pastry into a 10 cm sheet then cut 12 rounds out of it.
3. Place these rounds into each muffin cups and press them into these cups.
4. Transfer the muffin tray to the refrigerator and leave it for 20 minutes.
5. Add dried beans or pulses into each tart crust to add weight.
6. Transfer the muffin tray to the Ninja oven and Close its lid.
7. Rotate the Ninja Foodi dial to select the "Bake" mode.
8. Press the Time button and again use the dial to set the cooking time to 10 minutes.
9. Now press the Temp button and rotate the dial to set the temperature at 350 degrees F.
10. Now remove the dried beans from the crust and bake again for 10 minutes in the Ninja oven.

11. Meanwhile, prepare the filling beat beating butter with sugar and egg until fluffy.
12. Stir in flour and almonds ground then mix well.
13. Divide this filling in the baked crusts and top them with a tbsp. cherry jam.
14. Now again, place the muffin tray in the Ninja oven.
15. Continue cooking on the "Bake" mode for 20 minutes at 350 degrees F.
16. Whisk the icing sugar with 2 tbsp. water and top the baked tarts with sugar mixture.
17. Serve.

Nutrition:
- Calories: 398
- Fat: 13.8 g
- Carbs: 33.6 g
- Fiber: 1 g
- Sugar: 9.3 g
- Protein: 1.8 g

9. Brownie Bars

Preparation Time: 10 Minutes
Cooking Time: 28 Minutes
Servings: 8
Ingredients
Brownie

- 1/2 cup butter, cubed
- 1-oz. unsweetened chocolate
- 2 large eggs, beaten
- 1 tsp. vanilla extract
- 1 cup of sugar
- 1 cup flour, preferably all-purpose
- 1 tsp. baking powder
- 1 cup walnuts, chopped

Filling

- 6 oz. cream cheese softened
- 1/2 cup sugar
- 1/4 cup butter, softened
- 2 tbsp. all-purpose flour
- 1 large egg, beaten
- 1/2 tsp. vanilla extract

Topping

- 1 cup (6 oz.) chocolate chips
- 1 cup walnuts, chopped
- 2 cups mini marshmallows

Frosting

- 1/4 cup butter - 1/4 cup milk
- 2 oz. cream cheese
- 1-oz. unsweetened chocolate
- 3 cups confectioners' sugar
- 1 tsp. vanilla extract

Directions

1. In a small dish, add every ingredient for filling and whisk it until smooth.
2. Melt butter with chocolate in a large saucepan over medium heat.
3. Mix well, then remove the melted chocolate from the heat.
4. Now stir in vanilla, eggs, baking powder, flour, sugar, and nuts then mix well.
5. Spread this chocolate batter in the Ninja baking pan.
6. Drizzle nuts, marshmallows, and chocolate chips over the batter.
7. Place this baking pan in the Ninja oven and Close its lid.
8. Rotate the Ninja Food i dial to select the "Air Fry" mode.
9. Press the Time button and again use the dial to set the cooking time to 28 minutes.
10. Now press the Temp button and rotate the dial to set the temperature at 350 degrees F.
11. Meanwhile, prepare the frosting by heating butter with cream cheese, chocolate and milk in a saucepan over medium heat.
12. Mix well, then take it out from the heat.
13. Stir in vanilla and sugar, then mix well.
14. Pour this frosting over the brownie.
15. Allow the brownie to cool then slice into bars.
16. Serve.

Nutrition
- Calories: 271
- Fat: 15 g
- Carbs: 33 g
- Fiber: 1 g
- Sugar: 26 g
- Protein: 4 g

Chapter 5

Beef and Pork

1. Bourbon Pork Chops
Preparation Time: 5-10 minutes
Cooking Time: 20 minutes
Servings: 4
Ingredients
- 4 boneless pork chops - ¼ cup apple cider vinegar
- ¼ cup soy sauce - 3 tablespoons Worcestershire sauce
- 2 cups ketchup - ¾ cup bourbon
- 1 cup packed brown sugar

- ½ tablespoon dry mustard powder

Directions
1. Take Ninja Foodi Grill, orchestrate it over your kitchen stage, and open the top cover. Orchestrate the flame broil mesh and close the top cover.
2. Click "GRILL" and choose the "MED" grill function. Adjust the timer to 15 minutes and click "START/STOP."
3. Ninja Foodi is preheated and prepared to cook when it begins to signal. After you hear a signal, open the top.
4. Arrange the pork chops over the grill grate.
5. Close the top lid and cook for 8 minutes. Now open the top lid, flip the pork chops. Close the top lid and cook for 8 more minutes. Check the pork chops for doneness, cook for 2 more minutes if required. Coat the pork chops with salt and ground black pepper. Serve warm with the prepared sauce.

Nutrition
- Calories: 346 Fat: 13.5g Saturated Fat: 4g Trans Fat: 0g
- Carbohydrates: 27g Fiber: 0.5g Sodium: 1324mg Protein: 27g

2. Korean Chili Pork

Preparation Time: 5-10 minutes
Cooking Time: 8 minutes
Servings: 4

Ingredients
- 2 pounds pork, cut into ⅛-inch slices
- 5 minced garlic cloves
- 3 tablespoons minced green onion
- 1 yellow onion, sliced
- ½ cup soy sauce
- ½ cup brown sugar
- 3 tablespoons Korean red chili paste or regular chili paste
- 2 tablespoons sesame seeds
- 3 teaspoons black pepper
- Red pepper flakes to taste

Directions

1. Take a zip-lock bag, add all the ingredients. Shake well and refrigerate for 6-8 hours to marinate.
2. Take Ninja Foodi Grill, orchestrate it over your kitchen stage, and open the top.
3. Mastermind the barbecue mesh and close the top cover.
4. Click "GRILL" and choose the "MED" grill function. Flame broil work. Modify the clock to 8 minutes and afterward press "START/STOP." Ninja Foodi will begin to warm up.
5. Ninja Foodi is preheated and prepared to cook when it begins to signal. After you hear a signal, open the top.
6. Fix finely sliced pork on the barbeque mesh.
7. Cover and cook for 4 minutes. Then open the cover, switch the side of the pork. Cover it and cook for another 4 minutes.
8. Serve warm with chopped lettuce, optional.

Nutrition
- Calories: 621 Fat: 31g Saturated Fat: 12.5g Trans Fat: 0g
- Carbohydrates: 29g Fiber: 3g Sodium: 1428mg Protein: 53g

3. Lettuce Cheese Steak

Preparation Time: 5-10 minutes
Cooking Time: 16 minutes
Servings: 5-6
Ingredients
- 4 (8-ounce) skirt steaks
- 6 cups romaine lettuce, chopped
- ¾ cup cherry tomatoes halved
- ¼ cup blue cheese, crumbled
- Ocean salt and Ground Black Pepper
- 2 avocados, peeled and sliced
- 1 cup croutons - 1 cup blue cheese dressing

Directions
1. Coat steaks with black pepper and salt.
2. Take Ninja Foodi Grill, mastermind it over your kitchen stage, and open the top. Organize the barbecue mesh and close the top. Click "GRILL" and choose the "HIGH" function. Change the

clock to 8 minutes and afterward press "START/STOP." Ninja Foodi will begin pre-warming.
3. Ninja Foodi is preheated and prepared to cook when it begins to blare. After you hear a blare, open the top cover.
4. Fix finely the 2 steaks on the barbeque mesh.
5. Close the top cover and cook for 4 minutes. Presently open the top cover, flip the steaks. Close the top cover and cook for 4 additional minutes. Cook until the food thermometer comes to 165°F. Cook for 3-4 more minutes if needed. Grill the remaining steaks.
6. In a mixing bowl, add the lettuce, tomatoes, blue cheese, and croutons. Combine the ingredients to mix well with each other.
7. Serve the steaks warm with the salad mixture, blue cheese dressing, and avocado slices on top.

Nutrition:
- Calories: 576 Fat: 21g Saturated Fat: 8.5g Trans Fat: 0g
- Carbohydrates: 23g Fiber: 6.5g Sodium: 957mg Protein: 53.5g

4. Grilled Beef Burgers

Preparation Time: 5-10 minutes
Cooking Time: 10 minutes
Servings: 4
Ingredients
- 4 ounces cream cheese
- 4 slices bacon, cooked and crumbled
- 2 seeded jalapeño peppers, stemmed, and minced
- ½ cup shredded Cheddar cheese
- ½ teaspoon chili powder
- ¼ teaspoon paprika
- ¼ teaspoon ground black pepper
- 2 pounds ground beef
- 4 hamburger buns
- 4 slices pepper Jack cheese
- Optional - Lettuce, sliced tomato, and sliced red onion

Directions

1. In a mixing bowl, combine the peppers, Cheddar cheese, cream cheese, and bacon until well combined.
2. Prepare the ground beef into 8 patties. Add the cheese mixture onto four of the patties; arrange a second patty on top of each to prepare four burgers. Press gently.
3. In another bowl, combine the chili powder, paprika, and pepper. Sprinkle the mixture onto the sides of the burgers.
4. Take Ninja Foodi Grill, organize it over your kitchen stage, and open the top cover.
5. Organize the flame broil mesh and close the top cover.
6. Press "Flame broil" and select the "HIGH" barbecue work. Change the clock to 4 minutes and afterward press "START/STOP." Ninja Foodi will begin pre-warming.
7. Ninja Foodi is preheated and prepared to cook when it begins to blare. After you hear a blare, open the top. Arrange the burgers over the grill grate.
8. Close the top lid and allow it to cook until the timer reads zero. Cook for 3-4 more minutes, if needed.
9. Cook until the food thermometer reaches 145°F. Serve warm.
10. Serve warm with buns. Add your choice of toppings: pepper Jack cheese, lettuce, tomato, and red onion.

Nutrition
- Calories: 783
- Fat: 38g
- Saturated Fat: 16g
- Trans Fat: 0g
- Carbohydrates: 25g
- Fiber: 3g
- Sodium: 1259mg
- Protein: 57.5g

5. Espresso Marinated Chili Steak

Preparation Time: 10 minutes
Cooking Time: 50 minutes
Servings: 4
Ingredients

- 1 and ½ pounds beef flank steak
- 1-teaspoon instant espresso powder
- ½-teaspoon garlic powder
- 2 teaspoons chili powder
- 2 tablespoons olive oil
- Salt and pepper, to taste

Directions

1. Insert grill grate and close the hood
2. Pre-heat Ninja Foodi by pressing the "GRILL" option at and setting it to "HIGH" and timer to 40 minutes
3. Once it pre-heat until you hear a beep
4. Make the dry rub by mixing the chili powder, espresso powder, garlic powder, salt, and pepper
5. Rub all over the steak and brush with oil
6. Place on the grill grate and cook for 40 minutes
7. Flip after 20 minutes
8. Serve and enjoy!

Nutrition:

- Calories: 250
- Fat: 14 g
- Saturated Fat: 4 g
- Carbohydrates: 6 g
- Fiber: 2 g
- Sodium: 294 mg
- Protein: 20 g

6. Korean Chili Pork

Preparation Time: 10 minutes
Cooking Time: 8 minutes
Servings: 4
Ingredients

- 2 pounds pork, cut into 1/8-inch slices
- 5 garlic cloves, minced
- 3 tablespoons green onion, minced
- 1 yellow onion, sliced
- ½ cup of soy sauce
- ½-cup brown sugar
- 3 tablespoons Korean Red Chili Paste
- 2 tablespoons sesame seeds
- 3 teaspoons black pepper
- Red pepper flakes

Directions:

1. Take a zip bag and add listed ingredients, shake well and let it chill for 6-8 hours.
2. Pre-heat Ninja Foodi by pressing the "GRILL" option and setting it to "MED" and timer to 8 minutes.
3. Let it pre-heat until you hear a beep.
4. Arrange sliced pork over grill grate, lock lid and cook for 4 minutes.
5. Flip pork and cook for 4 minutes more, serve warm and enjoy with some chopped lettuce.

Nutrition:

- Calories: 620 Fat: 31 g
- Saturated Fat: 7 g Carbohydrates: 29 g
- Fiber: 3 g
- Sodium: 762 mg
- Protein: 58 g

7. Mustard Dredged Pork

Preparation Time: 10 minutes
Cooking Time: 30 minutes
Servings: 4
Ingredients

- 2 tablespoons ghee
- 2 tablespoons Dijon mustard
- 4 pork chops
- Salt and pepper to taste
- 1 tablespoon fresh rosemary, coarsely chopped

Directions

1. Take a bowl and add pork chops, cover with Dijon mustard and carefully sprinkle rosemary, salt, and pepper.
2. Let it marinate for 2 hours.
3. Add ghee and marinated pork chops to your Ninja Foodi pot.
4. Lock lid and cook on Low-Medium Pressure for 30 minutes.
5. Release pressure naturally over 10 minutes.
6. Take the dish out, serve, and enjoy!

Nutrition:

- Calories: 315
- Fat: 26g
- Saturated Fat: 8 g
- Carbohydrates: 1g
- Fiber: 0 g
- Sodium: 199 mg
- Protein: 18g

8. Jamaican Pork Dish

Preparation Time: 10 minutes
Cooking Time: 45 minutes
Servings: 4
Ingredients:
- ½ cup beef stock
- 1 tablespoon olive oil
- ¼ cup Jamaican jerk spice blend
- 4 ounces of pork shoulder

Directions:
1. Rub roast with olive oil and spice blend.
2. Set your Ninja Foodi to Sauté mode and add meat, brown all sides.
3. Pour beef broth.
4. Quick-release pressure.
5. Shred pork and serve!

Nutrition:
- Calories: 308
- Fat: 18g
- Saturated Fat: 6 g
- Carbohydrates: 5 g
- Fiber: 3 g
- Sodium: 210 mg
- Protein: 31 g

9. Tantalizing Beef Jerky

Preparation Time: 10 minutes
Cooking Time: 20 minutes
Servings: 4

Ingredients

- ½ pound beef, sliced into 1/8-inch-thick strips
- 2 tablespoons Worcestershire sauce
- 1 teaspoon onion powder
- ½ cup of soy sauce
- ½ teaspoon garlic powder
- 1 teaspoon salt
- 2 teaspoons ground black pepper

Directions

1. Take a large-sized Ziploc bag and add all the ingredients.
2. Seal it shut.
3. Lay strips on dehydrator trays, let not overlap them.
4. Close the air crisping lid.
5. Cook for 20 minutes to 135-degree F.
6. Serve and enjoy!

Nutrition

- Calories: 62
- Fat: 7g
- Saturated Fat: 2 g
- Carbohydrates: 2g
- Fiber: 0 g
- Sodium: 447 mg
- Protein: 9g

10. Spicy Adobo Steak

Preparation Time: 5 minutes
Cooking Time: 25 minutes
Servings: 4
Ingredients

- 2 cups of water
- 8 steaks, cubed, 28 ounces pack
- Pepper to taste
- 1 and ¾ teaspoons adobo seasoning
- 1 can (8 ounces) tomato sauce
- 1/3 cup green pitted olives
- 2 tablespoons brine
- 1 small red pepper
- ½ a medium onion, sliced

Directions

1. Chop onions and peppers into ¼ inch strips.
2. Season the beef with pepper and adobo.
3. Add into Ninja Foodi.
4. Add remaining ingredients and close the lid.
5. Cook for 25 minutes on HIGH.
6. Release pressure naturally.
7. Serve and enjoy!

Nutrition

- Calories: 154
- Fat: 5g
- Saturated Fat: 1 g
- Carbohydrates: 3g
- Fiber: 1 g
- Sodium: 700 mg
- Protein: 23g

11. Beef Stew

Preparation Time: 11 minutes
Cooking Time: 10 minutes
Servings: 4
Ingredients:
- 1-pound beef roast
- 4 cups beef broth
- 2 tomatoes, chopped
- ½ white onion, chopped
- 3 garlic cloves, chopped
- 1 carrot, chopped
- 2 celery stalks, chopped
- ¼ teaspoon salt
- 1/8 teaspoon ground black pepper

Direction
1. Add all ingredients to your Ninja Foodi.
2. Close the lid.
3. Cook for 10 minutes on HIGH.
4. Quick release pressure.
5. Serve and enjoy!

Nutrition
- Calories: 211
- Fat: 7g
- Saturated Fat: 2 g
- Carbohydrates: 2g
- Fiber: 0 g
- Sodium: 546 mg
- Protein: 10g

12. Lamb Roast

Preparation Time: 10 minutes
Cooking Time: 60 minutes
Servings: 4
Ingredients:

- 2 pounds lamb roasted Wegmans
- 1 cup beef broth
- 1 cup onion soup
- Salt and pepper to taste

Direction

1. Place your lamb roast to your Ninja Foodi pot.
2. Add beef broth, onion soup, salt and pepper.
3. Close the lid.
4. Cook for 55 minutes on Medium-HIGH.
5. Release pressure naturally over 10 minutes.
6. Serve and enjoy!

Nutrition

- Calories: 211
- Fat: 7g
- Saturated Fat: 2 g
- Carbohydrates: 2g
- Fiber: 1 g
- Sodium: 325 mg
- Protein: 10g

13. Mustard Pork

Preparation Time: 10 minutes
Cooking Time: 30 minutes
Servings: 4
Ingredients:
- 2 tablespoons ghee
- 2 tablespoons Dijon mustard
- 4 pork chops
- Salt and pepper to taste
- 1 tablespoon fresh rosemary, coarsely chopped

Directions:
1. Take a bowl and add pork chops, cover with Dijon mustard and carefully sprinkle rosemary, salt, and pepper.
2. Let it marinate for 2 hours.
3. Add ghee and marinated pork chops to your Ninja Foodi pot.
4. Lock lid and cook on Low-Medium Pressure for 30 minutes.
5. Release pressure naturally over 10 minutes/
6. Take the dish out, serve and enjoy!

Nutrition:
- Calories: 315
- Fat: 26g
- Saturated Fat: 8 g
- Carbohydrates: 1g
- Fiber: 0 g
- Sodium: 199 mg
- Protein: 18g

Chapter 6

Fish and Seafood

1. Subtly Roasted BBQ Shrimp

Preparation Time: 5-10 minutes
Cooking Time: 7 minutes
Servings: 2
Ingredients

- 3 tablespoons chipotle in adobo sauce, minced
- ¼-teaspoon salt

- ¼-cup BBQ sauce
- ½ orange, juiced
- ½-pound large shrimps

Directions
1. Take mixing bowl and add all ingredients, mix well
2. Keep it on the side
3. Pre-heat Ninja Foodi by pressing the "ROAST" option and setting it to "400 Degrees F" and timer to 7 minutes
4. Let it pre-heat until you hear a beep
5. Arrange shrimps over Grill Grate and lock lid, cook until the timer runs out
6. Serve and enjoy!

Nutrition
- Calories: 173 Fat: 2 g
- Saturated Fat: 0.5 g Carbohydrates: 21 g
- Fiber: 2 g
- Sodium: 1143 mg
- Protein: 17 g

2. Caper Sauce Dredged Sword Fish

Preparation Time: 10 minutes
Cooking Time: 8 minutes
Servings: 4
Ingredients:

- 4 swordfish steaks, about 1-inch thick
- 4 tablespoons unsalted butter
- 1 lemon, sliced into 8 slices
- 1-tablespoon lemon juice
- 1-tablespoon extra-virgin olive oil
- 2 tablespoons capers, drained
- Sea salt
- Black pepper, freshly grounded

Directions

1. Take a large shallow bowl and whisk together the lemon juice and oil.
2. Season with swordfish steaks with salt and pepper on each side, place in the oil mixture.
3. Turn to coat both sides and refrigerate for 15 minutes.
4. Insert the grill grate and close the hood.
5. Preheat Ninja Foodi by pressing the "GRILL" option at and setting it to "MAX" and timer to 8 minutes.
6. Let it preheat until you hear a beep.
7. Arrange the swordfish over the grill grate lock lid and cook for 9 minutes.
8. Place a medium saucepan over medium heat and melt butter.
9. Add the lemon slices and capers to the pan and cook for 1 minute. Then turn off the heat.
10. Remove the swordfish from the grill and serve with caper sauce over it. Enjoy!

Nutrition

- Calories: 472 Fat: 31 g Saturated Fat: 6 g Carbohydrates: 2 g
- Fiber: 0.5 g Sodium: 540 mg Protein: 48 g

3. Cool and Spicy Shrimp

Preparation Time: 10 minutes
Cooking Time: 7 minutes
Servings: 4
Ingredients:

- 1 and ¼ pound tiger shrimp, about 16-20 pieces
- ¼-teaspoon cayenne pepper
- ½ teaspoon old bay seasoning
- ¼ teaspoon smoked paprika
- 1 pinch of salt
- 1-tablespoon olive oil

Directions

1. Preheat Ninja Foodi by pressing the "AIR CRISP" option and setting it to "390 Degrees F" and timer to 10 minutes.
2. Take a mixing bowl and add ingredients (except shrimp), mix well.
3. Dip the shrimp into spice mixture and oil.
4. Transfer the prepared shrimp to your Ninja Foodi Grill cooking basket and cook for 5 minutes.
5. Serve and enjoy!

Nutrition:

- Calories: 170
- Fat: 2 g
- Saturated Fat: 0.5 g
- Carbohydrates: 5 g
- Fiber: 2 g
- Sodium: 1236 mg
- Protein: 23 g

4. Teriyaki Salmon and Vegetables

Preparation Time: 10 Minutes
Cooking Time: 15 Minutes
Servings: 4

Ingredients

- 4 (5-ounce) skin-on salmon fillets
- ½ teaspoon kosher salt (or ¼ teaspoon fine salt)
- 2 cups snow peas or snap peas
- ½ medium red bell pepper, cut into chunks
- ⅓ cup Teriyaki Sauce, plus 1 tablespoon - ¼ cup water
- 2 scallions, chopped - ½ cup Sautéed Mushrooms

Directions

1. Dash the salmon fillets with the salt and place them on the Reversible Rack set in the upper position.
2. Place the snow peas and bell pepper in the Foodi's™ inner pot. Drizzle with 1 tablespoon of teriyaki sauce and pour in the water. Place the rack with the salmon in the pot in the upper position. Seal the Pressure Lid into place, ensuring the valve is set to Seal. Choose Pressure; set the pressure to High and the cook time to 1 minute. Press Start. After cooking, use a quick pressure release. Carefully unlock and remove the Pressure Lid.
3. Brush about half the remaining ⅓ cup of teriyaki sauce over the salmon. Close the Crisping Lid and select Broil. Adjust the cook time to 7 minutes. Press Start. Check the salmon after 5 minutes. It should just flake apart when done. Cook for the remaining 2 minutes if necessary. Once done cooking, remove the rack with the salmon and set aside. Add the scallions and mushrooms to the vegetables in the pot and stir to heat through. If the sauce is too thin, select Sear/Sauté and adjust to High. Press Start. Simmer until the sauce is your preferred consistency. Distribute the vegetables among four plates and top with the salmon, drizzling the remaining teriyaki sauce over.

Nutrition

- Calories: 255 Total fat: 9g Saturated fat: 1g Cholesterol: 77mg
- Sodium: 1123mg Carbohydrates: 10g Fiber: 2g Protein: 32g

5. Shrimp and Vegetable Egg Rolls

Preparation Time: 10 Minutes
Cooking Time: 30 Minutes
Servings: 4
Ingredients:

- 2 tablespoons soy sauce
- 1 tablespoon dry sherry
- 2 teaspoons rice vinegar
- 3 cups shredded cabbage or coleslaw mix
- 3 scallions, chopped
- 1 large carrot, peeled and shredded
- 2 garlic cloves, minced
- 1 teaspoon grated peeled fresh ginger
- 1 teaspoon sugar
- 2 teaspoons sesame oil
- ¼ teaspoon freshly ground black pepper
- 8 ounces shrimp, peeled and coarsely chopped
- ½ cup Sautéed Mushrooms, coarsely chopped
- 1 teaspoon cornstarch
- 1 tablespoon water
- 8 to 10 egg roll wrappers
- Nonstick cooking spray, for cooking the egg rolls

Directions

1. In the Foodi's™ inner pot, combine the soy sauce, sherry, and rice vinegar. Add the cabbage, scallions, carrot, garlic, ginger, sugar, and sesame oil to the pot.
2. Seal the Pressure Lid into place, ensuring the valve is set to Seal. Choose Pressure; set the pressure to High and the cook time to 2 minutes. Press Start.
3. After cooking, use a quick pressure release. Carefully unlock and remove the Pressure Lid.
4. Add the pepper, shrimp, and mushrooms to the pot. Select Sear/Sauté and adjust to Medium-High. Press Start.

5. Bring the mixture to a simmer to cook the shrimp and warm the mushrooms. Continue simmering for about 5 minutes until most of the liquid has evaporated.
6. Take the filling to a bowl and set aside to cool. Wipe out the inner pot and return it to the base.
7. To form the egg rolls, in a small bowl, stir together the cornstarch and water. Lay a wrapper on your work surface positioned with a corner pointed toward you.
8. Mildly dampen the edges of the wrapper with the cornstarch mixture. Using a slotted spoon, scoop a scant ¼ cup of filling just below the center of the wrapper.
9. As you scoop the filling out, leave as much liquid behind as possible. You want the rolls to be dry inside, not soggy.
10. Fold the bottom corner of the wrapper over the filling and tuck it under the filling. Roll once and then fold both sides in. Continue to roll up tightly.
11. Repeat with the remaining wrappers and filling on the other side.
12. Close the Crisping Lid and select Air Crisp; adjust the temperature to 390°F and the time to 5 minutes to preheat. Press Start. Place 6 to 8 egg rolls in the Cook & Crisp™ Basket and spray with the cooking spray.
13. Flip them over and spray on all sides. When the pot has preheated, place the basket in the inner pot.
14. Close the Crisping Lid and select Air Crisp; adjust the temperature to 390°F and the cook time to 15 minutes.
15. Press Start. After 6 minutes, open the lid and check the egg rolls. They should be golden brown and crisp on top. If not, cook for an additional 1-2 minutes. Turn the rolls when the tops are crisp and cook for 5 to 6 minutes more or until crisp on the other side.
16. Repeat with any uncooked egg rolls. Allow the rolls cool on a wire rack for 8 to 10 minutes, as the interiors will be very hot. Serve with plum sauce, sweet and sour sauce, or Chinese mustard as desired.

Nutrition
- Calories: 181 Total fat: 4g Saturated fat: 1g Cholesterol: 87mg
- Sodium: 726mg Carbohydrates: 21g Fiber: 3g Protein: 17g

6. Clam Chowder with Parmesan Crackers

Preparation Time: 10 Minutes
Cooking Time: 30 Minutes
Servings: 4
Ingredients

- 2 cups oyster crackers
- 2 tablespoons melted unsalted butter
- ¼ cup finely grated Parmesan or similar cheese
- ½ teaspoon granulated garlic
- 1 teaspoon kosher salt (or ½ teaspoon fine salt), divided
- 2 thick bacon slices, cut into thirds
- 1 medium onion, chopped (about ¾ cup)
- 2 celery stalks, chopped (about ⅔ cup)
- 1 tablespoon all-purpose flour
- ¼ cup white wine
- 1 cup clam juice
- 3 (6-ounce) cans chopped clams, drained, liquid reserved
- 1 lb. Yukon Gold potatoes, cut into 1-inch chunks
- 1 teaspoon dried thyme leaves
- 1 bay leaf
- 1½ cups half-and-half
- 2 tablespoons chopped fresh parsley or chives

Directions

1. Close the Crisping Lid and select Air Crisp; adjust the temperature to 375°F and the time to 2 minutes to preheat. Press Start.
2. While the Foodi™ preheats, pour the oyster crackers into a medium bowl. Shower with the melted butter and sprinkle with the Parmesan, granulated garlic, and ½ teaspoon of kosher salt (or ¼ teaspoon of fine salt). Toss to coat the crackers. Transfer them to the Cook & Crisp™ Basket.
3. Once the pot is heated, open the Foodi's lid and insert the basket. Close the lid and select Air Crisp; adjust the temperature to

375°F and the cook time to 6 minutes. Press Start. Three minutes after, open the lid and stir the crackers. Close the lid and continue cooking until lightly browned and crisp. Take the basket and set aside to cool.

4. On your Foodi™, choose Sear/Sauté and adjust to Medium. Press Start. Let the pot preheat for 5 minutes. Put the bacon in the pot and cook for about 5 minutes, turning once or twice, until the bacon is crisp. Using tongs or a slotted spoon, transfer the bacon to a paper towel–lined plate to drain and set aside. Leave the fat in the pot.

5. Put in the celery and onion to the pot. Cook and stir for around a minute, until the vegetables begin to soften. Add in the flour and stir to coat the vegetables. Pour in the wine and bring to a simmer. Cook for about a minute or until reduced by about one-third. Add the clam juice, the reserved clam liquid (but not the clams), potatoes, remaining ½ teaspoon of kosher salt (or ¼ teaspoon of fine salt), thyme, and bay leaf.

6. Seal the Pressure Lid into place, ensuring the valve is set to Seal. Choose Pressure; set the pressure to High and the cook time to 4 minutes. Press Start.

7. Once done, let the pressure release naturally for 5 minutes, then quick release any remaining pressure. Carefully unlock and remove the Pressure Lid.

8. Stir in the clams and half-and-half. Select Sear/Sauté and adjust to Medium. Press Start. Bring the soup to a simmer to cook the clams through. Carefully remove the bay leaf. Serve the soup into bowls and crumble the bacon over the top. Garnish with the parsley and a handful of crackers, serving the remaining crackers on the side.

Nutrition

- Calories: 483 Total fat: 28g
- Saturated fat: 14g Cholesterol: 67mg
- Sodium: 989mg Carbohydrates: 47g
- Fiber: 5g Protein: 13g

7. Crab and Roasted Asparagus Risotto

Preparation Time: 10 Minutes
Cooking Time: 35Minutes
Servings: 4
Ingredients:

- 1 tablespoon olive oil
- 1 pound asparagus cut into 1-inch pieces
- 1 teaspoon kosher salt (or ½ teaspoon fine salt), divided
- 2 tablespoons unsalted butter
- 1 small onion, chopped (about ½ cup)
- 1 cup Arborio rice
- ⅓ cup white wine
- 2¾ to 3 cups Roasted Vegetable Stock or low-sodium vegetable broth
- 8 ounces lump crabmeat
- ⅓ cup grated Parmesan or similar cheese

Directions:

1. Close the Crisping Lid and select Air Crisp; adjust the temperature to 375°F and the time to 2 minutes to preheat. Press Start.
2. While the unit preheats, place the asparagus in the Cook & Crisp™ Basket. Drizzle with the olive oil. Sprinkle with ½ teaspoon of kosher salt (or ¼ teaspoon of fine salt) and toss.
3. Place the basket in the Foodi's™ inner pot. Close the Crisping Lid and select Air Crisp; adjust the temperature to 375°F and the cook time to 10 minutes. Press Start. After five minutes, open the lid and stir the asparagus, then continue cooking.
4. Once done cooking, remove the basket and set aside.
5. On your Foodi™, choose Sear/Sauté and set to Medium. Press Start. Add the butter to melt, and cook until it stops foaming. Add the onion. Cook for about 5 minutes, stirring, until it becomes softer. Add the rice, stir, and cook for about 1 minute. Add the wine. Cook for 2 to 3 minutes, stirring, until it's almost evaporated.

6. Add 2½ cups of vegetable stock and the remaining ½ teaspoon of kosher salt (or ¼ teaspoon of fine salt) and stir to combine.
7. Seal the Pressure Lid into place, ensuring the valve is set to Seal. Choose Pressure; set the pressure to High and the cook time to 8 minutes. Press Start.
8. After cooking, use a quick pressure release. Carefully unlock and remove the Pressure Lid.
9. Check the risotto; the rice should be soft with a slightly firm center and the sauce should be creamy, but it will probably not be quite done. If not, add another ¼ to ½ cup of stock. Select Sear/Sauté and adjust to Medium-Low. Press Start. Bring to a simmer then cook for 2 to 3 minutes until done. If the rice is done but too dry, add enough stock to loosen it up.
10. Gently stir in the asparagus and crabmeat and let it heat for a minute or so. Stir in the Parmesan. Taste and adjust the seasoning. Serve immediately.

Nutrition:
- Calories: 361
- Total fat: 11g
- Saturated fat: 4g
- Cholesterol: 44mg
- Sodium: 1435mg
- Carbohydrates: 45g
- Fiber: 4g
- Protein: 20g

8. Thai Fish Curry

Preparation Time: 10 Minutes
Cooking Time: 10 Minutes
Servings: 4
Ingredients:

- 1 (14-ounce) can coconut milk (not "lite")
- Vegetable or coconut oil, as needed
- 1 tbsp. Thai red curry paste, or to taste
- ½ cup seafood stock or water
- 1 medium zucchini, cut into ¼-inch rounds
- 1 small onion, sliced
- 1 pound frozen cod or grouper fillets
- 1 tsp. freshly squeezed lime juice (optional)
- 1 tsp. sugar (optional)
- 1 small (5-ounce) bag baby spinach
- 1 cup cherry tomatoes, halved
- 2 1 small red bell pepper cut into bite-size pieces
- tbsp. chopped fresh basil
- ¼ cup coarsely chopped roasted salted cashews

Directions

1. On your Foodi™, choose Sear/Sauté and set to Medium to preheat the inner pot. Select Start. Let the pot to preheat for 5 minutes.
2. Open the can of coconut milk without shaking it. Depending on the brand, you should see a thick layer of almost solid coconut "cream" on top. If yes, scoop out 2 to 3 tablespoons and add it to the inner pot. If no, add enough vegetable or coconut oil to the pot to form a thick coat on the bottom. Heat until shimmering. Add the curry paste and smash it down into the oil to fry it slightly, cooking for about 2 minutes. Mix in the remaining coconut milk and stir to dissolve.
3. Add the seafood stock, zucchini, onion, bell pepper, and fish fillets.

4. Seal the Pressure Lid into place, ensuring the valve is set to Seal. Select Pressure; set the pressure to Low and the cook time to 3 minutes. Press Start.
5. After cooking, use a quick pressure release. Carefully unlock and remove the Pressure Lid.
6. Using a fork, break the fish fillets into bite-size chunks. Taste the sauce. If needed, add the optional lime juice or sugar to balance the flavor.
7. Stir in the spinach and tomatoes to heat through. Serve over rice, if desired, garnished with the basil and cashews.

Nutrition
- Calories: 400
- Total fat: 29g
- Saturated fat: 22g
- Cholesterol: 42mg
- Sodium: 129mg
- Carbohydrates: 13g
- Fiber: 3g
- Protein: 26g

9. Blackened Salmon with Creamy Grits

Preparation Time: 10 Minutes
Cooking Time: 45 Minutes
Servings: 4

Ingredients

- ¾ cup grits (not instant or quick cooking)
- 1½ cups milk
- 1½ cups Chicken Stock, or store-bought low-sodium chicken broth
- 3 tbsp. unsalted butter, divided
- 2 tsp. kosher salt (or 1 tsp. fine salt), divided
- 3 tbsp. Cajun Seasoning Mix or store-bought mix
- 1 tbsp. packed brown sugar
- 4 (5-ounce) salmon fillets, skin removed
- Nonstick cooking spray

Directions

1. Pour the grits into a heat-proof bowl that holds at least 6 cups. Add the chicken stock, milk, 1 tablespoon of butter, and ½ teaspoon of kosher salt (or ¼ teaspoon of fine salt). Stir. Cover the bowl with aluminum foil.
2. Empty a cup of water into the inner pot. Put the Reversible Rack in the pot in the lower position and place the bowl on top.
3. Seal the Pressure Lid into place, ensuring the valve is set to Seal. Choose Pressure; set the pressure to High and the cook time to 15 minutes. Press Start.
4. While the grits cook, in a shallow bowl that fits one or two fillets at a time, stir together the seasoning, brown sugar, and remaining 1½ teaspoons of kosher salt (or ¾ teaspoon of fine salt).
5. Spray the fillets on one side with cooking spray and transfer one or two at a time, sprayed-side down, to the spice mixture. Spray the exposed sides of the fillets and turn over to coat that side in the seasoning. Repeat with the remaining fillets.
6. Once the grits cook, let the pressure release naturally for 10 minutes, then quick release any remaining pressure. Carefully unlock and remove the Pressure Lid.

7. Remove the rack and bowl from the pot. Add the remaining butter to the grits and stir to incorporate. Re-cover with the foil and return the bowl to the pot (without the rack).
8. Reverse the rack to the upper position. Put the salmon fillets on the rack and place the rack in the pot.
9. Close the Crisping Lid and choose Bake/Roast; set the temperature to 400°F and the cook time to 12 minutes. Press Start. After 6 minutes, open the lid and cautiously turn the fillets over. Close the lid and continue cooking. When the salmon is cooked and flakes easily with a fork, remove the rack. Remove the bowl of grits and uncover. Stir them again and serve immediately with the salmon.

Nutrition:
- Calories: 486
- Total fat: 22g
- Saturated fat: 9g
- Cholesterol: 111mg
- Sodium: 969mg
- Carbohydrates: 36g
- Fiber: 1g
- Protein: 36g

10. Salmon Cakes

Preparation Time: 10 Minutes
Cooking Time: 35 Minutes
Servings: 4
Ingredients:
- 1 pound fresh salmon
- 1 teaspoon kosher salt (or ½ teaspoon fine salt), divided
- 1 tablespoon unsalted butter
- 2 teaspoons olive oil
- 1 small onion, diced (about ½ cup)
- 1 large celery stalk, diced (about ½ cup)
- ½ small red bell pepper, diced (about ½ cup)
- ½ teaspoon Worcestershire sauce
- ¼ teaspoon hot pepper sauce
- 1 teaspoon Cajun Seasoning Mix or store-bought mix
- ¼ cup mayonnaise
- 1 teaspoon Dijon mustard
- 1 large egg, beaten
- ½ cup instant mashed potato flakes

Directions:
1. Sprinkle the salmon on both sides with ½ teaspoon of kosher salt (or ¼ teaspoon of fine salt) and place it on the Reversible Rack in the lower position. Pour a cup of water into the inner pot. Place the rack in the pot.
2. Seal the Pressure Lid into place, ensuring the valve is set to Seal. Choose Pressure; set the pressure to High and the cook time to 3 minutes. Press Start.
3. After cooking, use a quick pressure release. Carefully unlock and remove the Pressure Lid.
4. Remove the salmon and the rack and let the salmon rest until cool enough to handle. Take the water out of the pot and return the pot to the base.
5. Flake the salmon into a huge bowl and place it in the refrigerator. (If the salmon has skin, remove and discard it.)

6. On your Foodi™, choose Sear/Sauté and set to Medium to preheat the inner pot. Press Start. Let the pot to preheat for 5 minutes. Add the butter and oil. Once those ingredients stop foaming, add the onion, celery, and bell pepper. Sprinkle with the remaining ½ teaspoon of kosher salt (or ¼ teaspoon of fine salt). Stir to coat the vegetables in the fat and cook for 10 minutes, stirring occasionally.
7. Add the Worcestershire sauce, hot pepper sauce, and seasoning. Adjust the heat to Medium-High and cook for 2 minutes more.
8. Remove the salmon from the refrigerator and transfer the sautéed vegetables to the bowl.
9. In a small bowl, whisk the mayonnaise and mustard together. Whisk in the egg.
10. Put the mayonnaise mixture to the salmon and vegetables. Add the potato flakes. Gently but thoroughly mix the ingredients. Chill for 30 minutes.
11. Shape the mixture into four cakes. If you have egg rings, they come in very handy for shaping the cakes. If not, make the cakes about 1 inch thick and 3½ inches across.
12. Cover the Reversible Rack set in the upper position with nonstick aluminum foil (or regular foil sprayed with cooking spray). Carefully transfer the salmon cakes to the rack.
13. Close the Crisping Lid and choose Bake/Roast; set the temperature to 325°F and the time to 2 minutes to preheat. Press Start.
14. When the Foodi™ is preheated, place the rack and salmon into the pot. Close the Crisping Lid and choose Bake/Roast; leave the temperature at 325°F and adjust the cook time to 7 minutes. Press Start.
15. Once done cooking, select Broil and set the time for 4 minutes. Press Start. Cook until the top of the cakes are brown and crisp. Serve with a salad for a light dinner, or serve on buns with tartar sauce or the piquillo sauce for empanadas.

From Scratch
1. Make a spicy lemon butter sauce while the salmon cakes cook. Melt 2 tablespoons unsalted butter in a saucepan over low heat. Stir in 1 teaspoon Cajun Seasoning Mix or store-bought mix, and 1 tablespoon freshly squeezed lemon juice. Bring to a simmer and stir in a tablespoon heavy cream.

Nutrition:
- Calories: 332
- Total fat: 20g
- Saturated fat: 5g
- Cholesterol: 127mg
- Sodium: 590mg
- Carbohydrates: 13g
- Fiber: 1g
- Protein: 25g

Chapter 7

Poultry

1. Hearty Chicken Zucchini Kabobs

Preparation Time: 10 minutes
Cooking Time: 15 minutes
Servings: 4
Ingredients

- 1-pound chicken breast, boneless, skinless and cut into cubes of 2 inches
- 2 tablespoons Greek yogurt, plain

- 4 lemons juice
- 1 lemon zest
- ¼ cup extra-virgin olive oil
- 2 tablespoons oregano
- 1 red onion, quartered
- 1 zucchini, sliced
- 4 garlic cloves, minced
- 1 teaspoon of sea salt
- ½-teaspoon ground black pepper

Directions:
1. Take a mixing bowl, add the Greek yogurt, lemon juice, oregano, garlic, zest, salt, and pepper, combine them well
2. Add the chicken and coat well, refrigerate for 1-2 hours to marinate
3. Arrange the grill grate and close the lid
4. Pre-heat Ninja Foodi by pressing the "GRILL" option and setting it to "MED" and timer to 7 minutes
5. Take the skewers, thread the chicken, zucchini and red onion and thread alternatively
6. Let it pre-heat until you hear a beep
7. Arrange the skewers over the grill grate, lock lid and cook until the timer reads zero
8. Baste the kebabs with a marinating mixture in between
9. Take out your when it reaches 165 degrees F
10. Serve warm and enjoy!

Nutrition
- Calories: 277
- Fat: 15 g
- Saturated Fat: 4 g
- Carbohydrates: 10 g
- Fiber: 2 g
- Sodium: 146 mg
- Protein: 25 g

2. Sweet and Sour Chicken BBQ

Preparation Time: 10 minutes
Cooking Time: 40 minutes
Servings: 4
Ingredients:

- 6 chicken drumsticks
- ¾ cup of sugar
- 1 cup of soy sauce
- 1 cup of water
- ¼ cup garlic, minced
- ¼-cup tomato paste
- ¾ cup onion, minced
- 1-cup white vinegar
- Salt and pepper, to taste

Directions:

1. Take a Ziploc bag and add all ingredients into it
2. Marinate for at least 2 hours in your refrigerator
3. Insert the crisper basket, and close the hood
4. Pre-heat Ninja Foodi by pressing the "AIR CRISP" option at 390 degrees F for 40 minutes
5. Place the grill pan accessory in the air fryer
6. Flip the chicken after every 10 minutes
7. Take a saucepan and pour the marinade into it and heat over medium flame until sauce thickens
8. Brush with the glaze
9. Serve warm and enjoy!

Nutrition:

- Calories: 460 Fat: 20 g Saturated Fat: 5 g
- Carbohydrates: 26 g Fiber: 3 g
- Sodium: 126 mg Protein: 28 g

3. Delicious Maple Glazed Chicken

Preparation Time: 10 minutes
Cooking Time: 15 minutes
Servings: 4
Ingredients

- 2 pounds chicken wings, bone-in
- 1 teaspoon black pepper, ground
- ¼-cup teriyaki sauce
- 1-cup maple syrup
- 1/3 cup soy sauce
- 3 garlic cloves, minced
- 2 teaspoons garlic powder
- 2 teaspoons onion powder

Directions

1. Take a mixing bowl, add garlic, soy sauce, black pepper, maple syrup, garlic powder, onion powder, and teriyaki sauce, combine well
2. Add the chicken wings and combine well to coat
3. Arrange the grill grate and close the lid
4. Pre-heat Ninja Foodi by pressing the "GRILL" option and setting it to "MED" and timer to 10 minutes
5. Let it pre-heat until you hear a beep
6. Arrange the chicken wings over the grill grate, lock lid and cook for 5 minutes
7. Flip the chicken and close the lid, cook for 5 minutes more
8. Cook until it reaches 165 degrees F
9. Serve warm and enjoy!

Nutrition

- Calories: 543 Fat: 26 g
- Saturated Fat: 6 g Carbohydrates: 46 g
- Fiber: 4 g Sodium: 648 mg Protein: 42 g

4. Hot and Sassy BBQ Chicken

Preparation Time: 5-10 minutes
Cooking Time: 18 minutes
Servings: 4
Ingredients:

- 2 tablespoons honey
- 1-pound chicken drumstick
- 1-tablespoon hot sauce
- 2 cups BBQ sauce
- Juice of 1 lime
- Pepper and salt as needed

Directions

1. Take a bowl and add BBQ sauce, lime juice, honey, pepper, salt, hot sauce, and mix well
2. Take another mixing bowl, add ½-cup sauce and chicken mix well, and add remaining ingredients
3. Let it sit for 1 hour to marinate
4. Pre-heat Ninja Foodi by pressing the "GRILL" option and setting it to "MED" and timer to 18 minutes
5. Let it pre-heat until you hear a beep
6. Arrange chicken over grill grate, cook until the timer reaches zero and internal temperature reaches 165 degrees F
7. Serve and enjoy!

Nutrition

- Calories: 423
- Fat: 13 g
- Saturated Fat: 6 g
- Carbohydrates: 47 g
- Fiber: 4 g
- Sodium: 698 mg
- Protein: 22 g

5. Moroccan Roast Chicken

Preparation Time: 5-10 minutes
Cooking Time: 22 minutes
Servings: 4

Ingredients

- 3-tablespoon plain yogurt
- 4 skinless, boneless chicken thighs
- 4 garlic cloves, chopped
- ½-teaspoon salt
- 1/3 cup olive oil
- ½ teaspoon fresh flat-leaf parsley, chopped
- 2 teaspoons ground cumin
- 2 teaspoons paprika
- ¼ teaspoon crushed red pepper flakes

Directions

1. Take your food processor and add garlic, yogurt, salt, oil and blend well
2. Take a mixing bowl and add chicken, red pepper flakes, paprika, cumin, parsley, garlic, and mix well
3. Let it marinate for 2-4 hours
4. Pre-heat Ninja Foodi by pressing the "ROAST" option and setting it to "400 degrees F" and timer to 23 minutes
5. Let it pre-heat until you hear a beep
6. Arrange chicken directly inside your cooking pot and lock lid, cook for 15 minutes, flip and cook for the remaining time
7. Serve and enjoy with yogurt dip!

Nutrition

- Calories: 321 Fat: 24 g
- Saturated Fat: 5 g Carbohydrates: 6 g
- Fiber: 2 g Sodium: 602 mg Protein: 21 g

6. Classic Honey Soy Chicken

Preparation Time: 5-10 minutes
Cooking Time: 18 minutes
Servings: 4
Ingredients

- 4 boneless and skinless chicken breast then cut into small pieces
- 4 garlic cloves, smashed - 1 onion, diced
- ½-cup honey - 2-tablespoon lime juice
- 2-teaspoon sesame oil - 3-tablespoon soy sauce
- 1-tablespoon water - 1-tablespoon cornstarch
- 1-teaspoon rice vinegar Black pepper and salt to taste

Directions

1. In a mixing bowl, add the honey, sesame oil, lime juice, soy sauce, and rice vinegar. Combine well.
2. Take Ninja Foodi multi-cooker, arrange it over a cooking platform, and open the top lid.
3. In the pot, add the onion, chicken, and garlic; add the soy sauce mixture and stir gently.
4. Seal multi-cooker by locking it with the pressure lid; ensure to keep the pressure release valve locked/sealed.
5. Select "PRESSURE" mode and select the "HI" pressure level. Then, set timer to 15 minutes and press "STOP/START"; it will start the cooking process by building up inside pressure.
6. When timer goes off, quick release pressure by adjusting the pressure valve to the VENT. After pressure is release, open the pressure lid.
7. In a bowl, mix water and cornstarch until well dissolved.
8. Select "SEAR/SAUTÉ" mode and select the "MD" pressure level; add the cornstarch mixture in the pot and combine it. Stir-cook for 2 minutes. Serve warm.

Nutrition

- Calories: 493 Fat: 8.5g Saturated Fat: 1g
- Trans Fat: 0g Carbohydrates: 44.5g Fiber: 5g Sodium: 712mg
- Protein: 41.5g

7. Ninja Foodi BBQ Grilled Chicken

Preparation Time: 5 Minutes
Cooking Time: 30 Minutes
Servings: 4

Ingredients

- 2 c. barbecue sauce
- Juice of 1 lime
- 2 - tbsp. honey
- 1 - tbsp. hot sauce
- Kosher salt
- Freshly ground black pepper
- 1 lb. boneless skinless chicken breasts
- Vegetable oil, for grill

Directions

1. In an enormous bowl, whisk together grill sauce, lime juice, nectar, and hot sauce, and season with salt and pepper. Set aside ½ cup for seasoning.
2. Add chicken to a bowl and sling until covered.
3. Warmth Ninja Foodi oven broil to high. Oil meshes and Ninja Foodi oven broil chicken, seasoning withheld marinade, until roasted, 8MIN per side for bosoms, and 10 to 12MIN per side for drumsticks.

Nutrition

- Calories: 180
- Fat: 6g
- Carbohydrate: 6g
- Protein: 25g.

8. Ninja Foodi Crack BBQ Chicken

Preparation Time: 15 Minutes
Cooking Time: 2 Hours and 30 Minutes
Servings: 8
Ingredients:

- 1 - lb. boneless skinless chicken breasts
- 2 - c. water
- 2 - tbsp. kosher salt
- ¼ - c. brown sugar
- Kosher salt
- Freshly ground black pepper
- 1 - c. barbecue sauce
- Juice of 2 limes
- 2 - Cloves garlic, Minced

Directions:

1. Set the chook in a bib Ziploc sack and pound until ¼" thick. In a large mixing bowl, whisk collectively water, salt, and sugar until consolidated.
2. Pour the saline answer into Ziploc and refrigerate in any occasion 15MIN, yet preferably 2 HRS.
3. Take the chook out from brackish water and put off fluid.
4. Warmth barbeque to medium. Include chook and season with salt and pepper, at that point Ninja Foodi oven broil 6MIN consistent with aspect.
5. In an average size bowl, whisk together grill sauce, lime juice, and garlic. Treat fowl, flipping sometimes, till caramelized and cooked through.

Nutrition

- Calories: 122
- Fat: 11g
- Carbohydrate: 2g
- Protein: 20g

9. Ninja Foodi Sticky Grilled Chicken

Preparation Time: 10 Minutes
Cooking Time: 2 Hours and 35 Minutes
Servings: 4
Ingredients:

- ½ c. low-sodium soy sauce
- ½ c. balsamic vinegar
- 3 tbsp. honey
- 2 - Cloves garlic, Minced
- 2 - Green onions, thinly sliced
- 2½ lb. chicken drumsticks
- Vegetable oil, for grill
- 2 tbsp. sesame seeds, for garnish

Directions:

1. In an enormous bowl, whisk together soy sauce, balsamic vinegar, nectar, garlic, and green onions. Put aside ¼ cup marinade.
2. Add chicken to an enormous resalable plastic pack and pour it in the outstanding marinade. Let marinate in the cooler at any rate 2 HRS or up to expedite.
3. Once the barbecue is ready, heat Ninja Foodi oven broils to high. Oil meshes and barbecue chicken, seasoning with the held marinade and turning each 3 to 4MIN, until sang and cooked through, 24 to 30MIN aggregate.
4. Embellishment with sesame seeds before serving.

Nutrition

- Calories: 440
- Fat: 8g
- Carbohydrate: 51g
- Protein: 40g.

10. Ninja Foodi Grilled Chicken Breast

Preparation Time: 15 Minutes
Cooking Time: 30 Minutes
Servings: 4

Ingredients

- ¼ c. balsamic vinegar
- 3 - tbsp. extra-virgin olive oil
- 2 - tbsp. brown sugar
- 3 - Cloves garlic, Minced
- 1 - tsp. dried thyme
- 1 - tsp. dried rosemary
- 4 - Chicken breasts
- Kosher salt
- Freshly ground black pepper
- Freshly chopped parsley, for garnish

Directions

1. In an average size bowl, mix balsamic vinegar, olive oil, earthy colored sugar, garlic, and dried herbs altogether, and season liberally with salt and pepper. Hold ¼ cup.
2. Add bird to the bowl and hurl to sign up for. Let marinate in any occasion 20MIN and up to expedite.
3. Preheat Ninja Foodi oven broil to medium-high. Include hen and Ninja Foodi oven broil, treating with saved marinade, until cooked through, 6MIN according to facet.
4. Embellishment with parsley earlier than serving.

Nutrition

- Calories: 208
- Fat: 4g
- Carbohydrate: 6g
- Protein: 0g.

11. Ninja Foodi Grilled Pineapple Chicken

Preparation Time: 10 Minutes
Cooking Time: 2 Hours and 10 Minutes
Servings: 4

Ingredients

- 1 c. - unsweetened pineapple juice
- ¾ c. - ketchup
- ½ c. - low-sodium soy sauce
- ½ c. brown sugar
- 2 - Cloves garlic, Minced
- 1 - tbsp. freshly Minced ginger
- 1 lb. - boneless skinless chicken breasts
- 1 - tsp. vegetable oil, plus more for the grill
- 1 - Pineapple, sliced into rings & halved
- Thinly sliced green onions, for garnish

Directions:

1. In an enormous bowl, whisk together pineapple juice, ketchup, soy sauce, earthy colored sugar, garlic, and ginger until joined.
2. Add chicken to an enormous plastic pack and pour in the marinade. Let marinate in the refrigerator in any event 2 Hours and up to expedite.
3. At the point when prepared to barbecue, heat Ninja Foodi oven broil to high. Oil meshes and Ninja Foodi oven broil chicken, seasoning with marinade, until scorched and cooked through, 8MIN per side.
4. Sling pineapple with oil and Ninja Foodi oven broil until burned, 2MIN per side.
5. Topping chicken and pineapple with green onions before serving.

Nutrition

- Calories: 171 Fat: 1g Carbohydrate: 12g Protein: 27g

12. Ninja Foodi Grilled Chicken Wings

Preparation Time: 10 Minutes
Cooking Time: 25 Minutes
Servings: 4
Ingredients:

- Zest of 1 lemon - 2 - tsp. kosher salt
- 1 - tsp. smoked paprika
- 1 - tsp. garlic powder
- 1 - tsp. onion powder
- 1 - tsp. dried thyme
- ¼ tsp. cayenne - 2 lb. - chicken wings
- Vegetable oil, for the grill

For The Sauce

- ½ c. mayonnaise - Juice of 1 lemon
- 1 - tbsp. Dijon mustard - 2 - tsp. horseradish
- 2 - tsp. freshly chopped chives
- 1 - tsp. hot sauce, such as Crystal

Directions:

1. In an average size bowl, whisk together lemon get-up-and-go, salt, paprika, garlic powder, onion powder, thyme, and cayenne. Pat chicken wings dry and see in a big bowl. Add taste combination and sling to cover.
2. Warm Ninja Foodi oven broil or barbeque dish to medium warm temperature. Oil Ninja Foodi oven broil grates with vegetable oil. Include wings and cook, mixing on occasion, till the skin is fresh and meat is cooked via 15 to 20 minutes.
3. In the period in-between, make the sauce: In an average size bowl, whisk collectively mayo, lemon juice, mustard, horseradish, chives, and hot sauce.
4. Serve wings hot with plunging sauce.

Nutrition:

- Calories: 129 Fat: 7g Carbohydrate: 5g Protein: 10g

Chapter 8

Vegetarian

1. Vegetable Pasta Delight

Preparation Time: 5-10 Minutes
Cooking Time: 15 Minutes
Servings: 2-3
Ingredients

- 1 small zucchini, sliced
- 1 small sweet yellow, halved
- 2/3 cups orzo pasta, cooked and drained
- ¼ pound fresh asparagus, trimmed
- 1 small Portobello mushroom, stem removed
- 1/2 small red onion, halved

Dressing

- 2 tablespoons balsamic vinegar
- 1 ½ tablespoons lemon juice
- 2 garlic cloves, minced
- 1 tablespoon olive oil
- ½ teaspoon lemon-pepper seasoning

Salad
- ½ tablespoon minced parsley
- ½ tablespoon minced basil
- 1/4 teaspoon salt
- ½ cup grape tomatoes, halved
- 1/8 teaspoon pepper
- ½ cup (2 ounces) feta cheese, crumbled

Directions
1. In two separate bowls, combine all the salad and dressing ingredients.
2. Take Ninja Foodi Grill, place it over your kitchen stage, and open the top cover.
3. Arrange the grill grate and Close it lid.
4. Press "GRILL" and choose the "MED" grill function. Set the timer to 10 minutes and then press "START/STOP." Ninja Foodi will start pre-heating.
5. Ninja Foodi is preheated and prepared to cook when it begins to beep. After you hear a signal, open the top.
6. Arrange the mushrooms, pepper, and onion over the grill grate.
7. Close it cover and cook for 5 minutes. Now open the top cover, flip the vegetables.
8. Close it cover and cook for 5 more minutes.
9. Grill the other vegetables in the same manner with 2 minutes per side for the zucchini and asparagus.
10. Dice the grilled vegetables; add them to the salad bowl. Add the pasta and top with the dressing; toss and serve.

Nutrition
- Calories: 234
- Fat: 14g
- Saturated Fat: 1g
- Trans Fat: 0g
- Carbohydrates: 38g
- Fiber: 4g
- Sodium: 369mg
- Protein: 12g

2. Creamy Corn Potatoes

Preparation Time: 5-10 Minutes
Cooking Time: 30-40 Minutes
Servings: 4

Ingredients

- 1 1/2 pound red potatoes, quartered and boiled
- 3 tablespoons olive oil
- 1 tablespoon cilantro, minced
- 2 sweet corn ears, without husks
- 1/4 teaspoon cayenne pepper
- 2 poblano peppers
- 1/2 cup milk
- 1 teaspoon ground cumin
- 1 tablespoon lime juice
- 1 jalapeno pepper, seeded and minced
- 1/2 cup sour cream
- 1 ½ teaspoons garlic salt

Directions

1. Drain the potatoes and rub them with oil.
2. Take Ninja Foodi Grill, place it over your kitchen stage, and open the top cover.
3. Arrange the grill grate and Close it lid.
4. Press "GRILL" and choose the "MED" grill function. Set the timer to 10 minutes and then press "START/STOP." Ninja Foodi will start pre-heating.
5. Ninja Foodi is preheated and prepared to cook when it begins to beep. After you hear a signal, open the top.
6. Arrange the poblano peppers over the grill grate.
7. Close it cover and cook for 5 minutes. Now open the top cover, flip the peppers.
8. Close it cover and cook for 5 more minutes.
9. Grill the other vegetables in the same manner with 7 minutes per side for the potatoes and corn.
10. Whisk the remaining ingredients in another bowl.

11. Peel the grilled pepper and chop them. Divide corn ears into smaller pieces and cut the potatoes as
12. Serve the grilled veggies with the vinaigrette on top.

Nutrition
- Calories: 322
- Fat: 4.5g
- Saturated Fat: 1g
- Trans Fat: 0g
- Carbohydrates: 51.5g
- Fiber: 3g
- Sodium: 600mg
- Protein: 5g

3. Spinach Chickpea Stew

Preparation Time: 5-10 Minutes
Cooking Time: 5 Minutes
Servings: 5-6
Ingredients

- 4 sweet potatoes, peeled and diced
- 4 cups vegetable broth
- 1 tablespoon extra-virgin olive oil
- 1 yellow onion, diced
- 4 garlic cloves, minced
- 4 cups baby spinach
- 2 (15-ounce) cans chickpeas, drained
- 1 (15-ounce) can fire-roasted diced tomatoes, undrained
- 1 teaspoon ground coriander
- ½ teaspoon black pepper, freshly ground
- ½ teaspoon paprika
- ½ teaspoon sea salt
- 1 ½ teaspoons ground cumin

Directions

1. Take Ninja Foodi multi-cooker, arrange it over a cooking platform, and open the top lid.
2. In the pot, add the oil; Select "SEAR/SAUTÉ" mode and select "MD: HI" pressure level.
3. Press "STOP/START." After about 4-5 minutes, the oil will start simmering.
4. Add the onions, garlic, and cook (while stirring) until they become softened and translucent.
5. Add the sweet potatoes, broth, tomatoes, chickpeas, cumin, coriander, paprika, salt, and black pepper; stir the mixture.
6. Seal the multi-cooker by locking it with the pressure lid; ensure to keep the pressure release valve locked/sealed.
7. Select "PRESSURE" mode and select the "HI" pressure level. Then, set timer to 8 minutes and press "STOP/START"; it will start the cooking process by building up inside pressure.

8. Once the timer goes off, fast release pressure by adjusting the pressure valve to the VENT. After pressure gets released, open the pressure lid.
9. Select "SEAR/SAUTÉ" mode and select the "MD" pressure level; add the spinach and combine. Stir-cook until wilts.
10. Serve warm and enjoy!

Nutrition
- Calories: 234
- Fat: 4.5g
- Saturated Fat: 0g
- Trans Fat: 0g
- Carbohydrates: 39.5g
- Fiber: 9g
- Sodium: 576mg
- Protein: 8g

4. Cheese Stuffed Zucchini

Preparation Time: 5-10 Minutes
Cooking Time: 8 Minutes
Servings: 2
Ingredients:

- 5 ounces Parmesan, shredded
- ½ teaspoon chili flakes
- ¼ teaspoon dried basil
- 1 zucchini
- ½ teaspoon tomato paste
- 1 teaspoon olive oil

Directions

1. Take the zucchini; cut into halves. Scoop the flesh from them and spread with the tomato paste inside the hollowed halves.
2. Add the shredded cheese. Sprinkle with the chili flakes, dried basil, and olive oil.
3. Take Ninja Foodi multi-cooker, arrange it over a cooking platform, and open the top lid.
4. In the pot, arrange a reversible rack and place the Crisping Basket over the rack.
5. In the basket, add the zucchini halves.
6. Seal the multi-cooker by locking it with the crisping lid; ensure to keep the pressure release valve locked/sealed.
7. Select the "AIR CRISP" mode and adjust the 375°F temperature level. Then, set timer to 8 minutes and press "STOP/START"; it will start the cooking process by building up inside pressure.
8. Once the timer goes off, fast release pressure by adjusting the pressure valve to the VENT.
9. After pressure gets released, open the pressure lid. Serve warm and enjoy!

Nutrition

- Calories: 326 Fat: 21g Saturated Fat: g Trans Fat: 0g
- Carbohydrates: 6.5g Fiber: 1g Sodium: 458mg Protein: 12.5g

5. Broccoli Crisp

Preparation Time: 5-10 Minutes
Cooking Time: 15 Minutes
Servings: 4
Ingredients

- ½ teaspoon red pepper flakes
- ¼ cup toasted sliced almonds
- 1 large heads broccoli, cut into florets
- 2 tablespoons extra-virgin olive oil
- Black pepper (ground) and salt to taste
- 2 tablespoons grated Parmesan cheese
- Lemon wedges, for serving

Directions

1. In a mixing bowl, add the broccoli and toss it with the olive oil. Season with salt and black pepper. Add the red pepper flakes and toss to combine.
2. Take Ninja Foodi multi-cooker, arrange it over a cooking platform, and open the top lid.
3. In the pot, arrange a reversible rack and place the Crisping Basket over the rack.
4. In the basket, add the broccoli mixture.
5. Seal the multi-cooker by locking it with the crisping lid; ensure to keep the pressure release valve locked/sealed.
6. Select the "AIR CRISP" mode and adjust the 390°F temperature level. Then, set timer to 15 minutes and press "STOP/START"; it will start the cooking process by building up inside pressure. Once the timer goes off, fast release pressure by adjusting the pressure valve to the VENT.
7. After pressure gets released, open the pressure lid. Mix in the almonds. Serve warm with the cheese on top and lemon wedges and enjoy!

Nutrition

- Calories: 181 Fat: 11.5g Saturated Fat: 3g Trans Fat: 0g
- Carbohydrates: 9g Fiber: 4g Sodium: 421mg Protein: 7.5g

6. Mashed Asparagus

Preparation Time: 5-10 Minutes
Cooking Time: 10 Minutes
Servings: 2
Ingredients:

- 1 tablespoon butter
- 1 teaspoon cayenne pepper
- ½ teaspoon chili pepper
- 3 cups vegetable broth
- 16 ounces asparagus, chopped
- ½-⅓ cup sour cream
- 1 teaspoon paprika
- 1 tablespoon sriracha
- 2 teaspoons salt

Directions:

1. Take Ninja Foodi multi-cooker, arrange it over a cooking platform, and open the top lid.
2. In the pot, add the chopped asparagus, cayenne pepper, salt, and broth
3. Seal the multi-cooker by locking it with the pressure lid; ensure to keep the pressure release valve locked/sealed.
4. Select "PRESSURE" mode and select the "HI" pressure level. Then, set timer to 10 minutes and press "STOP/START"; it will start the cooking process by building up inside pressure.
5. Once the timer goes off, fast release pressure by adjusting the pressure valve to the VENT. After pressure gets released, open the pressure lid.
6. Add the asparagus in a food processor or blender. Add the chile pepper, butter, sriracha, and sour cream. Blend the mixture until it becomes smooth.
7. Serve warm and enjoy!

Nutrition

- Calories: 86 Fat: 8.5g Saturated Fat: 1g Trans Fat: 0g
- Carbohydrates: 5g Fiber: 1.5g Sodium: 386mg Protein: 4g

7. Apple Green Salad

Preparation Time: 5-10 Minutes
Cooking Time: 6 Minutes
Servings: 2-3

Ingredients

- 1/4 teaspoon Sriracha chili sauce
- 2 tablespoons cilantro, chopped
- 1/4 cup blue cheese, crumbled
- 1 apple, wedged
- 2 tablespoons orange juice
- 3 tablespoons avocado oil
- 1 tablespoon honey
- 1/4 teaspoon salt - 2 tablespoons vinegar
- ½ garlic clove, minced - 5 ounces salad greens

Directions

1. In a mixing bowl, put the chili sauce, orange juice, oil, honey, vinegar, cilantro, garlic, and salt and mix. Add 1/4th on the dressing with the apples in another bowl; toss well.
2. Take Ninja Foodi Grill, place it over your kitchen stage, and open the top cover. Arrange the grill grate and Close it lid.
3. Press "GRILL" and choose the "MED" grill function. Set the timer to 6 minutes and then press "START/STOP." Ninja Foodi will start pre-heating. Ninja Foodi is preheated and prepared to cook when it begins to beep. After you hear a signal, open the top.
4. Arrange the apples over the grill grate.
5. Close it cover and cook for 3 minutes. Now open the top cover, flip the apples. Close it cover and cook for 3 more minutes.
6. Combine other ingredients in another bowl. Add the apples and top with the remaining dressing. Serve warm.

Nutrition:

- Calories: 406 Fat: 5g Saturated Fat: 1.5g Trans Fat: 0g
- Carbohydrates: 48g Fiber: 3g Sodium: 517mg Protein: 2g

8. Spinach Olive Meal

Preparation Time: 5-10 Minutes
Cooking Time: 15 Minutes
Servings: 5-6

Ingredients

- 2/3 cup Kalamata olives, halved and pitted
- 1 ½ cups feta cheese, grated
- 4 tablespoons butter
- 2 pounds spinach, chopped and boiled
- Ground black pepper and salt to taste
- 4 teaspoons grated lemon zest

Directions

1. In a mixing bowl, add the spinach, butter, salt, pepper.
2. Take Ninja Foodi multi-cooker, arrange it over a cooking platform, and open the top lid.
3. In the pot, arrange a reversible rack and place the Crisping Basket over the rack.
4. In the basket, add the spinach mixture.
5. Seal the multi-cooker by locking it with the crisping lid; ensure to keep the pressure release valve locked/sealed.
6. Select the "AIR CRISP" mode and adjust the 340°F temperature level. Then, set timer to 15 minutes and press "STOP/START"; it will start the cooking process by building up inside pressure.
7. Once the timer goes off, fast release pressure by adjusting the pressure valve to the VENT.
8. After pressure gets released, open the pressure lid.
9. Serve warm and enjoy!

Nutrition

- Calories: 253 Fat: 18g
- Saturated Fat: 3g Trans Fat: 0g
- Carbohydrates: 8g Fiber: 4g Sodium: 339mg Protein: 10.5g

Chapter 9

Desserts

1. Creamy Mango Cake
Preparation Time: 5-10 minutes
Cooking Time: 30 minutes
Servings: 8-10
Ingredients

- 2 cups white flour - 1/2 cup sugar
- 2 mangoes, peeled and cubed
- 6 eggs, whisked - 1 cup heavy cream
- 1 teaspoon vanilla extract - 1 teaspoon baking powder

Directions

1. Take a cake pan, grease it with some cooking spray, vegetable oil, or butter. Add the ingredients and combine well.
2. Take Ninja Foodi multi-cooker, arrange it over a cooking platform, and open the top lid. In the pot, add water and place a reversible rack inside the pot. Place the pan over the rack. Close the multi-cooker by

locking it with the Crisping Lid, ensure to keep the pressure release valve locked/sealed.
3. Select "BAKE/ROAST" mode and adjust the 350°F temperature level. After that set timer to 30 minutes, then press "STOP/START," it will start the cooking process by building up inside pressure. Once the timer goes off, quickly release pressure by adjusting the pressure valve to the VENT.
4. When the pressure gets released, open the Crisping Lid. Slice the cake and serve warm.

Nutrition
- Calories: 301 Fat: 14g Saturated Fat: 7g Trans Fat: 0g
- Carbohydrates: 26.5g Fiber: 2g Sodium: 153mg Protein: 6g

2. Easy Pineapple Cake
Preparation Time: 5-10 minutes
Cooking Time: 40 minutes
Servings: 8-10
Ingredients
- 2 ounces chocolate chips
- 12 ounces canned pineapple, crushed
- 14 ounces cake mix

Directions:
1. Take a cake pan, grease it with some cooking spray, vegetable oil, or butter. Add the ingredients and combine well.
2. Take Ninja Foodi multi-cooker, arrange it over a cooking platform, and open the top lid.
3. In the pot, add water and place a reversible rack inside the pot. Place the pan over the rack.
4. Close the multi-cooker by locking it with the Crisping Lid, ensure to keep the pressure release valve locked/sealed.
5. Select "BAKE/ROAST" mode and adjust the 350°F temperature level. After that, set timer to 40 minutes then press "STOP/START," it will start the cooking process by building up inside pressure.
6. Once the timer goes off, quickly release pressure by adjusting the pressure valve to the VENT.
7. When the pressure gets released, open the Crisping Lid. Slice the cake and serve warm.

Nutrition
- Calories: 258 Fat: 8g

- Saturated Fat: 1g Trans Fat: 0g
- Carbohydrates: 36g
- Fiber: 3g
- Sodium: 125mg
- Protein: 3g

3. Chocolate Pudding

Preparation Time: 5-10 minutes
Cooking Time: 20 minutes
Servings: 4

Ingredients

- 2 eggs, whisked
- 2 teaspoons butter, melted
- 1 cup dark chocolate, melted
- 16 ounces cream cheese
- 2 tablespoons sugar

Directions

1. Take 4 ramekins, grease it with some cooking spray, vegetable oil, or butter. In a bowl, whisk all the ingredients and add in the ramekins.
2. Take Ninja Foodi multi-cooker, arrange it over a cooking platform, and open the top lid.
3. In the pot, add water and place a reversible rack inside the pot. Place the pan over the rack.
4. Close the multi-cooker by locking it with the Crisping Lid, ensure to keep the pressure release valve locked/sealed.
5. Select "BAKE/ROAST" mode and adjust the 340°F temperature level. After that, set the timer to 20 minutes then press "STOP/START," it will start the cooking process by building up inside pressure.
6. Once the timer goes off, quickly release pressure by adjusting the pressure valve to the VENT.
7. When the pressure gets released, open the Crisping Lid. Slice the cake and serve warm.

Nutrition:

- Calories: 523 Fat: 28g Saturated Fat: 11g
- Trans Fat: 0g Carbohydrates: 44g
- Fiber: 2g Sodium: 421mg Protein: 12g

4. Chocolate Peanut Butter and Jelly Puffs

Preparation Time: 25 minutes
Cooking Time: 15 minutes
Servings: 4

Ingredients

- 1 (16-ounce) tube prepared flaky biscuit dough
- 2 (1½-ounce) milk chocolate bars
- Cooking spray
- 16 teaspoons (about ⅓ cup) creamy peanut butter
- 1 cup confectioners' sugar
- 1 tablespoon whole milk
- ¼ cup raspberry jam

Directions

1. Remove biscuits from tube. There is a natural width-wise separation in each biscuit. Gently peel each biscuit in half using this separation.
2. Break the chocolate into 16 small pieces.
3. Spray a baking sheet with cooking spray.
4. Using your hands, stretch a biscuit half until it is about 3-inches in diameter. Place a teaspoon of peanut butter in center of each biscuit half, then place piece of chocolate on top.
5. Pull an edge of dough over the top of the chocolate and pinch together to seal. Continue pulling the dough over the top of the chocolate and pinching until the chocolate is completely covered. The dough is pliable, so gently form it into a ball with your hands.
6. Place on the prepared baking sheet. Repeat this step with the remaining biscuit dough, peanut butter, and chocolate.
7. Place the baking sheet in the refrigerator for 5 minutes.
8. Place Cook & Crisp Basket in pot. Close crisping lid. Choose Air Crisp, fix temperature to 360°F, and time to 20 minutes. Select Start/Stop to begin. Let preheat for 5 minutes.
9. Remove the biscuits from the refrigerator and spray the tops with cooking spray. Open lid and spray the basket with cooking spray.
10. Place 5 biscuit balls in the basket. Close lid and cook for 5 minutes.
11. When cooking is complete, remove the biscuit balls from the basket. Repeat step 7 two more times with remaining biscuit balls.
12. Mix together the confectioners' sugar, milk, and jam in a small bowl to make a frosting.

13. When the cooked biscuit balls are cool enough to handle, dunk the top of each into the frosting. As frosting is beginning to set, garnish with any toppings desired, such as sprinkles, crushed toffee or candy, or mini marshmallows.

Nutrition
- Calories: 663
- Total Fat: 25g
- Saturated Fat: 8g
- Cholesterol: 5mg
- Sodium: 1094mg
- Carbohydrates: 101g
- Fiber: 3g
- Protein: 14g

5. Red Velvet Cheesecake

Preparation Time: 10 minutes
Cooking Time: 25 minutes
Servings: 8
Ingredients:

- 2 cups Oreo cookie crumbs
- 3 tablespoons unsalted butter, melted
- 2 packages cream cheese, at room temperature
- ½ cup granulated sugar - ½ cup buttermilk
- 2 tablespoons unsweetened cocoa powder
- 1 teaspoon vanilla extract - 2 tablespoons red food coloring
- ½ teaspoon white vinegar - 1 cup water

Directions:

1. In a small bowl, blend the cookie crumbs and butter. Press this mixture into the bottom of the Ninja Multi-Purpose Pan or 8-inch baking pan. In a huge bowl, use an electric hand mixer to blend the cream cheese, sugar, buttermilk, cocoa powder, vanilla, food coloring, and vinegar for 3 minutes. Pour this over the cookie crust. Cover the pan tightly with aluminum foil.
2. Place the water in the pot. Insert Reversible Rack into pot, making sure it is in the lower position. Place the covered multi-purpose pan onto the rack. Attach pressure lid, ensuring the pressure release valve is in the SEAL position.
3. Select PRESSURE on HI. Set time to 25 minutes. Press Start/Stop to begin. Once done cooking, let the pressure to naturally release for 15 minutes. After 15 minutes, quick release any pressure remaining by turning the pressure release valve to the VENT position. Cautiously remove lid when unit has finished releasing pressure. Remove cheesecake from the pot. Leave in the refrigerator for 3 hours, or overnight if possible before serving.

Nutrition

- Calories: 437 Total Fat: 31g Saturated Fat: 18g
- Cholesterol: 74mg Sodium: 338mg Carbohydrates: 36g
- Fiber: 3g Protein: 7g

6. Black Beans Brownies

Preparation Time: 10 minutes
Cooking Time: 20 minutes
Servings: 12

Ingredients
- 4 oz. Chocolate, chopped.
- 4 eggs; whisked.
- 1 cup white flour
- ½ cup canned black beans; drained, and blended
- ½ cup butter, melted
- ¼ cup brewed black coffee
- 1 ¼ cups sugar
- 1 tsp. vanilla extract
- Cooking spray

Directions
1. In a bowl, put and combine all the ingredients except the cooking spray and whisk well.
2. Grease a cake pan with the cooking spray and pour the batter in it
3. Put the reversible rack in the Foodi, add the cake pan inside, set the machine on Baking mode, and cook at 350°F for 20 minutes. Slice the brownies and serve.

Nutrition
- Calories: 233 kcal
- Protein: 5.52 g
- Fat: 11.64 g
- Carbohydrates: 26.58 g

7. Cocoa and Orange Pudding

Preparation Time: 10 minutes
Cooking Time: 20 minutes
Servings: 4
Ingredients

- 1 egg
- 2 tbsp. orange juice
- 4 tbsp. white flour
- 1 tbsp. cocoa powder
- 4 tbsp. sugar
- 2 tbsp. coconut oil, melted
- 4 tbsp. Milk
- ½ tsp. Baking powder
- ½ tsp. Lime zest; grated.

Directions

1. In a bowl, mix all the ingredients, stir well and divide into 4 ramekins.
2. Put the reversible rack in the Foodi, put the ramekins inside, set the machine on Baking mode, and cook 320 for 20 minutes. Serve the pudding warm.

Nutrition

- Calories: 188 kcal
- Protein: 5.42 g
- Fat: 11.48 g
- Carbohydrates: 16.93 g

8. Apple Pie

Preparation Time: 5 minutes
Cooking Time: 55 minutes
Servings: 8

Ingredients

- 2 apples, cored, peeled and sliced
- 2 eggs; whisked.
- ¾ cup milk
- 2/3 cup white flour
- 1/3 cup sugar
- Cooking spray
- 2 tbsp. flavored liqueur
- 1 tsp. cinnamon powder

Directions

1. In a bowl, mix the sugar with the cinnamon, flour, eggs, milk, and the liqueur and stir well.
2. Grease the Foodi's cake pan with cooking spray and arrange the apples into the pan
3. Pour the batter over the apples and put the pan in the Foodi.
4. Set the machine on Baking mode and cook at 400°F for 55 minutes. Cool the pie down, slice, and serve.

Nutrition

- Calories: 136 kcal
- Protein: 5.07 g
- Fat: 4.1 g
- Carbohydrates: 20.16 g

9. Apple Jam

Preparation Time: 10 minutes
Cooking Time: 20 minutes
Servings: 6

Ingredients

- 1 lb. apples, peeled, cored and chopped
- 2 lbs. sugar
- 2 cups apple juice
- Juice of 2 limes

Directions

1. In your Foodi, combine all the ingredients, toss, put the pressure lid on and cook on High for 20 minutes.
2. Blend the mixture using an immersion blender, divide into cups and serve cold.

Nutrition

- Calories: 683 kcal
- Protein: 1.41 g
- Fat: 1.26 g
- Carbohydrates: 171.87 g

10. Pineapple and Yogurt Cake

Preparation Time: 10 minutes
Cooking Time: 40 minutes
Servings: 6
Ingredients:
- 5 oz. flour
- 1 egg; whisked.
- ½ cup sugar
- 1/3 cup coconut flakes, shredded
- ¼ cup pineapple juice
- 4 tbsp. vegetable oil
- 3 tbsp. yogurt
- ¾ tsp. baking powder
- ½ tsp. baking soda
- ½ tsp. cinnamon powder
- Cooking spray

Directions:
1. In a bowl, put and mix all the ingredients except the cooking spray and whisk well. Grease the Foodi's cake pan with cooking spray and pour the cake batter inside
2. Put the reversible rack in the Foodi, put the cake pan on the rack, set the machine on baking mode, and cook the cake at 320°F for 40 minutes. Cool down, cut, and serve it.

Nutrition:
- Calories: 267 kcal
- Protein: 5.47 g
- Fat: 13.49 g
- Carbohydrates: 31.4 g

Chapter 10

Extra Recipes

1. Tomato Salsa
Preparation Time: 5-10 minutes
Cooking Time: 10 minutes
Servings: 4
Ingredients: 1 red onion, peeled, cut in quarters
- 1 jalapeño pepper, cut in half, seeds removed
- 5 Roma tomatoes, cut in half lengthwise
- 1-tablespoon kosher salt - 2 teaspoons ground black pepper
- 2 tablespoons canola oil - 1 bunch cilantro, stems trimmed
- Juice and zest of 3 limes - 3 cloves garlic, peeled
- 2 tablespoons ground cumin

Directions
1. In mixing bowl, combine onion, tomatoes, jalapeño pepper, salt, black pepper, and canola oil. Take Ninja Foodi Grill, arrange it over kitchen platform, and open top lid. Arrange grill grate and close the top lid.
2. Press "GRILL" and select the "MAX" grill function. Adjust the timer to 10 minutes and then press "START/STOP." Ninja Foodi start preheating. Ninja Foodi preheated and ready to cook when starts to beep. After you, hear a beep, open top lid.
3. Arrange vegetables over the grill grate. Close top lid and cook for 5 minutes. Now open the top lid, flip the vegetables. Close the top lid and cook for five more minutes. Blend the mixture in a blender and serve as needed.

Nutrition
- Calories: 169 Fat: 9g Saturated Fat: 2g Trans Fat: 0g
- Carbohydrates: 12g Fiber: 3g Sodium: 321mg Protein: 2.5g

2. Potato Corn Chowder

Preparation Time: 5-10 minutes
Cooking Time: 50 minutes
Servings: 4
Ingredients
- 3 tablespoons unsalted butter - 1 small onion, finely chopped
- 4 ears corn, shucked - 2 tablespoons canola oil
- 1 ½ teaspoons sea salt - ½ teaspoon freshly ground black pepper
- 4 cups diced potatoes - 2 cups half-and-half
- 2 ½ cups vegetable broth - 1 ½ cups milk
- 1 ½ teaspoon chopped fresh thyme

Directions
1. Brush the corn ears with ½ tablespoon of oil. Season corn with salt and black pepper.
2. Take Ninja Foodi Grill, arrange it over kitchen platform, and open top lid. Arrange grill grate and close the top lid.
3. Press "GRILL" and select "MAX" grill function. Adjust the timer to 12 minutes and then press "START/STOP." Ninja Foodi will start preheating.
4. Ninja Foodi preheated and ready to cook when it starts to beep. After you, hear a beep, open top lid.

5. Arrange corn over the grill grate. Close the top lid and cook for 6 minutes. Now open the top lid, flip the corn. Close the top lid and cook for 6 more minutes. Cut the kernels from the cobs.
6. In a blender or food processor, purée 1 cup of corn kernels until smooth.
7. Sauté the onions in a saucepan with some butter. Add the broth, milk, and potatoes. Simmer for 10 to 12 minutes. Add the pureed corn, remaining corn kernels, and half-and-half, salt, and black pepper. Stir the mixture and cook for about 15-20 minutes. Blend the corn mixture; serve with the thyme on top.

Nutrition
- Calories: 523 Fat: 28g Saturated Fat: 11g Trans Fat: 0g
- Carbohydrates: 56g Fiber: 8g Sodium: 711mg Protein: 13g

3. Mushroom Tomato Roast

Preparation Time: 10 minutes
Cooking Time: 15 min
Servings: 4
Ingredients
- 2 cups cherry tomatoes
- 2 cups cremini, button, or other small mushrooms
- 1/4 cup red wine/Sherry vinegar
- 2 garlic cloves, finely chopped
- 1/2 cup extra-virgin olive oil
- 3 tablespoons chopped thyme
- Pinch of crushed red pepper flakes
- 1-teaspoon kosher salt
- 1/2 teaspoon black pepper
- 6 scallions, cut crosswise into 2-inch pieces

Directions:
1. Take a zip-lock bag; add black pepper, salt, red pepper flakes, thyme, vinegar, oil, and garlic. Add mushrooms, tomatoes, and scallions.
2. Shake well and refrigerate for 30-40 minutes to marinate.
3. Take Ninja Foodi Grill, arrange it over kitchen platform, and open top lid.
4. Press, "BAKE" and adjust the temperature to 400°F. Adjust the timer to 12 minutes and press "START/STOP." Ninja Foodi start preheating.

5. Ninja Foodi preheated and ready to cook when starts to beep. After you, hear a beep, open top lid.
  6. Arrange mushroom mixture directly inside the pot.
  7. Close the top lid and allow it to cook until the timer reads zero.
  8. Serve warm.

Nutrition
- Calories: 253 Fat: 24g Saturated Fat: 4g Trans Fat: 0g
- Carbohydrates: 7g Fiber: 2g Sodium: 546mg Protein: 1g

4. Cheddar Cauliflower Meal

Preparation Time: 5-10 minutes
Cooking Time: 15 minutes
Servings: 2

Ingredients
- ½-teaspoon garlic powder
- ½-teaspoon paprika
- Sea salt, ground black pepper to taste
- 1 head cauliflower, stemmed and leaves removed
- 1 cup Cheddar cheese, shredded
- Ranch dressing, for garnish
- ¼ cup canola oil or vegetable oil
- 2 tablespoons chopped chives
- 4 slices bacon, cooked and crumbled

Directions
  1. Cut the cauliflower into 2-inch pieces.
  2. In a mixing bowl, add the oil, garlic powder, and paprika. Season with salt and ground black pepper; combine well. Coat the florets with the mixture.
  3. Take Ninja Foodi Grill, arrange it over kitchen platform, and open top lid. Arrange grill grate and close the top lid.
  4. Press "GRILL" and select "MAX" grill function. Adjust the timer to 15 minutes and then press "START/STOP." Ninja Foodi will start preheating.
  5. Ninja Foodi preheated and ready to cook when it starts to beep. After you hear a beep, open the top lid.
  6. Arrange pieces over the grill grate.
  7. Close the top lid and cook for 10 minutes. Now open the top lid, flip the pieces and top with the cheese.

8. Close top lid and cook for 5 more minutes. Serve warm with the chives and ranch dressing on top.

Nutrition
- Calories: 534 Fat: 34g Saturated Fat: 13g Trans Fat: 0g
- Carbohydrates: 14.5g Fiber: 4g Sodium: 1359mg Protein: 31g

5. Buttery Spinach Meal

Preparation Time: 10 minutes
Cooking Time: 15 minutes
Servings: 4

Ingredients
- 2/3 cup Kalamata olives, halved and pitted
- 1 and ½ cups feta cheese, grated
- 4 tablespoons butter
- 2 pounds spinach, chopped and boiled
- Pepper and salt to taste
- 4 teaspoons lemon zest, grated

Directions
1. Take a mixing bowl, add spinach, butter, salt, pepper, and mix well
2. Pre-heat Ninja Foodi by pressing the "AIR CRISP" option and setting it to "340 Degrees F" and timer to 15 minutes
3. Let it pre-heat until you hear a beep
4. Arrange a reversible trivet in the Grill Pan, arrange spinach mixture in a basket and place basket in the trivet
5. Let them roast until the timer runs out
6. Serve and enjoy!

Nutrition
- Calories: 250
- Fat: 18 g
- Saturated Fat: 6 g
- Carbohydrates: 8 g
- Fiber: 3 g
- Sodium: 309 mg
- Protein: 10 g

6. Turkey Dip

Preparation Time: 10 minutes
Cooking Time: 25 minutes
Servings: 6

Ingredients

- 1 and ½ pound turkey meat, ground
- 2 carrots, chopped
- 4 garlic cloves, minced
- 2 cups tomato puree
- 1 yellow onion, chopped
- 1 tablespoon olive oil
- Salt and black pepper to the taste

Directions

1. Set the Foodi on Sauté mode, add the oil, heat it up, add the onion and the garlic and sauté for 5 minutes.
2. Add the rest of the ingredients, place the pressure lid on and cook on High for 20 minutes.
3. Release the pressure freely for 10 minutes, divide everything into bowls and serve.
4. Serve with your favorite pasta.

Nutrition

- Calories: 200
- Fat: 14g
- Fiber: 6g
- Carbs: 17g
- Protein: 8g

7. Sweet Potato Dip

Preparation Time: 10 minutes
Cooking Time: 20 minutes
Servings: 6
Ingredients
- 3 cups canned tomatoes, crushed
- 3 garlic cloves, minced
- 2 cups sweet potato, chopped
- Salt and black pepper to the taste

Directions
1. In your Foodi, mix all the ingredients, put the pressure lid on and cook on High for 20 minutes.
2. Release the pressure freely for 10 minutes, blend the mix using an immersion blender, divide into bowls and serve.

Nutrition
- Calories: 171
- Fat: 9g
- Fiber: 6g
- Carbs: 17g
- Protein: 9g

8. Apple Dip

Preparation Time: 10 minutes
Cooking Time: 15 minutes
Servings: 4
Ingredients

- 8 apples, cored and chopped
- ½ cup water
- 1 teaspoon cinnamon powder

Directions

1. In your Foodi, combine all the ingredients, put the pressure lid on and cook on High for 15 minutes.
2. Release the pressure freely for 10 minutes, blend the mix with an immersion blender, divide the dip into bowls and serve cold.

Nutrition

- Calories: 131
- Fat: 7g
- Fiber: 6g
- Carbs: 9g
- Protein: 4g

9. Orange Cranberry Dip

Preparation Time: 10 minutes
Cooking Time: 15 minutes
Servings: 4

Ingredients

- 2 and ½ teaspoons orange zest
- 12 ounces cranberries
- ¼ cup orange juice
- 4 tablespoons maple syrup

Directions

1. In your Foodi, mix all the ingredients, put the pressure lid on and cook on High for 15 minutes.
2. Release the pressure freely for 10 minutes, blend the dip with an immersion blender, divide into bowls and serve.

Nutrition

- Calories: 135
- Fat: 3g
- Fiber: 6g
- Carbs: 8g
- Protein: 4g

10. Chili Basil Dip

Preparation Time: 5 minutes
Cooking Time: 8 minutes
Servings: 6

Ingredients

- 5 red chilies, seedless and chopped
- 3 garlic cloves, crushed
- Salt and black pepper to the taste
- ½ cup veggie stock
- 1 bunch basil, chopped
- 2 tablespoons balsamic vinegar

Directions

1. In your Foodi, mix all the ingredients, put the pressure lid on and cook on High for 8 minutes.
2. Release the pressure freely for 5 minutes, blend using an immersion blender, divide the mix into bowls and serve.

Nutrition

- Calories: 120
- Fat: 5g
- Fiber: 3g
- Carbs: 9g
- Protein: 4g

Conclusion

Thank you for making it through to the end of Ninja Foodi Grill Cookbook. How does it feel reading all these preparations? Let's hope it was informative and provide you with all the tools you need to get started serving up delicious and nutritious dishes in minutes.

Even though the Ninja Foodi does the job of many appliances in one, it doesn't impinge on the quality of its cooks. If you're craving chicken breasts with crispy skin, the Ninja Foodi will do just that. If you are aiming for juicy, tender pork, you can have that too.

Each function of the Ninja Foodi has particular settings, and therefore, it's important to get familiar with the functions before you start to cook with it. It's a good idea to read through the instructional manual as you explore the settings. Be sure to clean the cooker thoroughly before using it for the first time, and then clean it after each use. Don't use tools or utensils that will scratch the pot.

When you first use the Ninja Foodi, it's best to start with a simple recipe to practice using the functions. Remember to always do a pressure test before your first use to make sure the machine works properly. This will also help you become familiar with the different settings.

The main intention of the Ninja Foodi is to make your cooking life as easy and hassle-free as possible. What's wonderful is that you don't need to worry about the meal overcooking while you're asleep. If you set your food to cook for 8 hours, it will automatically shut off after that time and stay warm for several hours.

There are so many delicious recipes in this book, but they're just the beginning. As you become more acquainted with the Ninja Foodi, try out other recipes or experiment with the ones in this book. The more you use the Ninja Foodi, the easier it will become and the more comfortable you will be trying new recipes.

The next step is to start using the recipes you have learned. Everybody is different, and that includes taste as well, so you will have to figure out what works best for you. The most important thing is to make sure that you spend time with your family, enjoying cooking and eating. Do things together and ensure that you all like doing them.

You're encouraged to start using your Ninja Foodi now. Don't let it gather dust in the corner of the kitchen. Use it as often as you wish, and like many people online, you may find you can't live without it! All the best!